simply
fun
for families

simply
fun
for families

GWEN ELLIS

Revell
Grand Rapids, Michigan

Published by Fleming H. Revell
a division of Baker Publishing Group
P.O. Box 6287, Grand Rapids, MI 49516-6287

Material in this book originally appeared in *The Big Book of Family Fun* (© 1999), *Finding Dollars for Family Fun* (© 1993), *Finding Time for Family Fun* (© 1991), and *Raising Kids on Purpose for the Fun of It* (© 1989).

Printed in the United States of America

Library of Congress Cataloging-in-Publication Data
Ellis, Gwen, 1938–
      Simply fun for families / Gwen Ellis.
            p.   cm. — (The big book of family fun)
      ISBN 0-8007-5988-5
      1. Parenting—United States. 2. Parents—Time management—United States.
      3. Family recreation—United States. 4. Child rearing—United States. I. Title.
      II. Series.
      HQ755.8E384 2005
      649′.1—dc22   2004028083

contents

5

Part III: Getting Out and About as a Family

introduction

families, start your engines!

Ideas not coupled with action never become bigger than the brain cells they occupied.

Arnold H. Glasow

At the writing of this book, gasoline prices have skyrocketed out of sight. People are afraid to drive anywhere they don't absolutely have to go. They are putting vacation plans on hold. In our area, hotels, hurt by the lack of tourists, are advertising that they will pay for a tank of gas if you will just stay in their facilities. Who knows where gas prices will be when you actually sit down to read this book? But whether they are high or low, if you want to go far away or stay near home, this book will give you many ideas for finding family fun right in your own neighborhood and everywhere else you care to go.

7

I have put together a ton of ideas to help you find quality time with your family. You probably couldn't use all these ideas in a lifetime, but if you can use even a few of them, that is worth the price you paid for the book.

My mother used to tell me, "If you want to have fun, you have to put forth a little effort." So many things our mothers tell us turn out to be true, and this saying did too. It is only by getting out the bikes, strapping on the backpacks, getting together a picnic lunch, or buying tickets to an event that we start the wheels turning for a great family time. In most cases, we have to show the initiative to look for family fun. Fun ideas rarely come looking for us. Our biggest challenge is overcoming the inertia that makes us want to be couch potatoes more than anything else. But if we are going to use play as a way to bond as a family, give our kids a childhood to remember, and save money and have fun doing it, we will have to be somewhat intentional about looking for ideas and doing the planning to make play happen.

> "If you want to have fun, you have to put forth a little effort."

The good news is that if you keep this book on a nearby shelf while your children are growing up and refer to it again and again, you will have more ideas for fun than you'll have time to do. For many adventures, this book is only a starting place. You'll probably need to do research to see if your family's wish list for fun fits your finances and interests. If you live in Iowa, you are not going to be able to build sand castles beside the sea unless you go to the sea, and that involves expense. You are probably not going to be able to visit a dairy farm if you live in midtown Manhattan. But no matter where you live, there is something special about your place.

I have provided many websites where you can do research. Of course, all of these websites also have links to other websites, and you can go on and on researching. Just remember that in whatever little valley or mountaintop town you live, there are wonderful things to explore and unique places to go that will give every family member a memorable moment and help tie your family unit together more tightly. So let's get started.

Now, before the protests begin that you don't have time and you don't have money for a family vacation, I have also included lots of ideas for saving time and money every day so that you *can* give your kids those memorable times in family life. The time-savers are identified by an hourglass ⧗, and the money-saving tips are identified by a dollar sign $. They are at the end of every chapter. When the lists had too much valuable information for the end of a chapter, I put them in an appendix at the back of the book.

So are you ready to read and learn how to save both time and money and build family memories?

part I
get set for fun

the importance
of taking time to play

Have you ever watched running, screaming, laughing young children on a playground? Looks like an ant's nest that's been stirred up, doesn't it? The kids' actions seem pretty loose and random. It doesn't look as though much thought is going into what happens next. And that is true. But visit a playfield of an older group of children, and you'll find a highly structured form of play. Often it is some kind of sports activity—soccer, softball, or basketball. There are rules to be followed, and cooperation becomes a necessity for a team to win the game.

For both age groups, play is the most important work they have to do. It is the business of kids. For the young child, his world expands as he imagines, explores, and learns to get along with other kids. The older child learns discipline, cooperation, and sportsmanship. Play equals learning. It is the child's life work.

See How They Grow

Here's a thumbnail sketch of what to expect with regard to play.

● *Infancy*: Babies begin to be interested in play during the first year of life. First it is independent play in which the infant bangs a toy or turns a wheel. The infant learns by experimenting. For example, you drop something, and it falls down. She tries it once, likes the effect, and tries it again. She has learned something useful to her. The child doesn't know that a ball will roll until either someone demonstrates or the child accidentally tries it. The child first experiments and then makes the learning a part of his or her life.

It will be a while before the child begins to play with others. But as young as six months

14

of age, an infant begins to reach out to others to touch, smile, and exchange babbling.

- *Toddlers*: As young as two years of age, it is common for a child to act out everyday life—cooking at a toy stove, dressing up to go shopping, and playing house. Because our children are so visually stimulated by television, you will often find them acting out a favorite television character.

- *Early childhood*: Play for the three- to six-year-old is simple, repetitive, big-muscle activities such as running around a room or rolling a toy back and forth. At the early end of the age group, the young child prefers to play independently but is happy to be near a playmate. This kind of play is called "parallel play." Somewhere between ages two and four, curiosity hits a lifetime high. A three-year-old can ask hundreds of questions in a day. Curiosity can be used to great advantage in learning through play.

- *School-age children*: School-age children begin to interact with others, and eventually they progress toward organized games with rules and common goals. All young children learn by actual contact with things and people. While a great deal of learning can take place

15

from books and television, it is best to plan family activities that include getting out to see and do things together.

Just Play with Me

Your job as a parent, grandparent, or caregiver is to provide a rich environment in which the child can play in safety. Perhaps this means arranging a play date for him, getting down on the floor and playing with him, or providing him equipment and toys. Whether you are called upon to spend money or time on a child, it is the best investment you will ever make.

I'm glad I learned to play, and I'm especially glad I learned to play with my children. When I think of the places we've been and the experiences we've shared, my memories are very sweet. There are many things families can do together that are so much fun. You can walk on an ocean beach, camp on the top of a mountain, walk in a valley in the rain, and visit zoos and game farms. You can go to amusement parks and sporting events. You can visit historical sites and travel to far-off places. You can swim or play in the mud or

> **The whole world is yours, and you can explore it all again as you play with a child.**

build sand castles. You can watch a movie or go to a play or visit a rose garden. The whole world is yours, and you can explore it all again as you play with a child.

You don't have to know very much to play with a child. Children are experts on play and will teach you. Give any child some sunshine, water, and time, and he can amuse himself for hours. Children will be happiest if you are there too, helping build a dam across a small stream, laughing, talking, planning how to build the dam even bigger, and then plotting how you are going to "crash it down."

Play doesn't have to be elaborate or complicated. What a child wants is you and your undivided attention. She wants you to be there—not only your body, but your eyes, your heart, and your mind. Is it too much to ask? You may fool some people into thinking you are paying attention to them, but you will never fool a child.

What Are You Thinking, Child?

If you want to know what a child is thinking, if you care about what he is learning to believe, spend time with him. Playtime is a wonderful time for finding out what's going

17

on in his head and heart. It's a great time to uncover fears and misconceptions that may have been planted there by something a playmate said, a program he's seen on television, or conversations he has heard between grownups that he really didn't understand. It's a great time to plant your values and beliefs in his heart. Unlike the formal classroom where information is passed along, most of it by rote, playtime is a place to follow the biblical admonition to:

> Impress them [the commands, decrees, and laws of the LORD] on your children. Talk about them when you sit at home and when you walk along the road, when you lie down and when you get up.
>
> Deuteronomy 6:7 NIV

Most important principles of life are passed on to a new generation not by what you say, but by what you show in your life. Playtime is a time to teach spiritual lessons. Values and priorities can be taught best in the course of everyday living, and wise caregivers learn to take advantage of every opportunity to point out the goodness of God, his provision, and the difference between right and wrong. You see, more learning is caught than taught.

Not only parents but grandparents too can play a huge role in influencing their youngsters in citizenship, moral character, and spiritual development—even if the children live far away. My own children's grandfather was a tower of strength in their young lives. Whether he was teaching them how to pan for gold in a Montana stream, plant a garden, or care for an animal, he was influencing them for good. His consistent character, lived out before them, was a powerful witness to a life of quality and character. They watched him plunk his tithes in the offering plate. They heard his kind response to the downtrodden. They listened to his stories of the faithfulness of God. They saw him give up something he really wanted to do, just to be with them. They saw him show love and compassion right up to the last days of his life. That kind of influence is very powerful in the developing life of a child.

So, What Keeps Us from Playing with Our Kids?

There are all kinds of reasons why we don't play with our kids. We are too busy, we are too tired, we are not interested, we can't afford it, or we don't know how to play anymore. Probably the last excuse, not knowing how to play anymore, is the most honest one we offer. So this entire book is devoted to ideas for how you and your family can play together. We will provide hundreds of ideas that are *Simply Fun for Families.*

Somehow most of us have made play a chore, one more thing on our "to do" list, but it

19

doesn't have to be. You could use playtime with a child as a time to rediscover your own life. You could pick up on some of the things you missed growing up and share those experiences with a growing child. It could be the best thing that ever happened to both of you.

I'm the new grandmother (I promise I won't brag too much) of a little girl. At this writing, she lives all the way across the continent from me, and I don't get to see her nearly often enough. But when I do, we play. I sneeze on purpose, and she laughs. I tickle her tummy, and she squirms. I show her how to put her toes in her mouth, and she thinks that's just great. Our play is simple and fulfilling for both of us. Later on, I hope to take her to the ocean and help her find seashells and watch as the waves crash on the beach. We'll build sand castles and dig holes, and I'm sure I will have as much fun as she will.

We'll start simply and build our adventures. Maybe someday she and I can go to India to see how people live there or take the elevator to the top of the Eiffel Tower to gaze on all of Paris spread out below us. Maybe we'll read stories by a campfire or bake special cookies for her mommy. That won't be work—not for me anyway. It will just be way too much fun for both of us.

God gave each of us exactly the amount of time we need for our lives.

So if you want to do one thing to enhance your relationship with your kids, to build family ties, and to have lots of fun—play with your kids. You'll never regret a single moment you spend with them.

How to Find Time for Family Fun

In these sections of the book, we're going to talk about time. I'll be offering ideas for saving time, but first, we need to talk about our attitude toward time.

What does the number 168 mean to you? It's an important number for everyone. It's the number of hours in a week. Every living person gets the same number of hours each week. God gave each of us exactly the amount of time we need for our lives. It doesn't feel that way most of the time, but it's true. How well we plan and how well we use our allotted time has a lot to do with how much time we have for family fun.

Let's take a look at the ways we use a week of time:

| Sleep | 8 hours x 7 days a week | 56 hours |
| Grooming | 2 hours x 7 days a week | 14 hours |

(Before you say, "I don't spend that much time grooming," think of the time spent getting haircuts, manicuring your nails, running to the dry cleaners, etc.)

21

Work, school	8 hours x 5 days a week	40 hours

(Many people spend much more time at work than 40 hours.)

Commuting	7 hours (plus or minus)	7 hours
Food-related activities	3 hours a day x 7 days a week	21 hours
Total		**138 hours**

Okay, you do the math: you have thirty hours a week left over to do what you please. Suppose you choose to spend three hours a night watching television, for a total of twenty-one hours a week. Now you have nine hours left. Even nine hours a week is better than nothing, and nine hours, if carefully planned, can be a good chunk of time for relating as family members.

So here are the foundational ideas about time.

● Get rid of guilt. Be realistic about your time situation.

    a. If you are a single parent, you won't have as many hours for family fun as others may. Learn to make the time you do have the best it can be by giving yourself wholly to it.

    b. If you're a traveling parent and are gone more than you're home, you have to accept that time limitation with your family and determine to make the time you do have with your kids the best possible.

22

    c. If you are a stay-at-home parent, but your plate is full of tasks, analyze what's really important in your life. It may be time to cut out some of those seemingly important tasks.

    d. If you're an 8-to-5 job parent, but you have tons of work to haul out of your briefcase every night, accept it and give yourself wholly to your kids when you *are* relating to them. Promise yourself that you will give them some quality time every day, even if it is only a story at bedtime.

- Learn to use bits of time to relate to your kids. That's what this section of the book is about as well. Also check out the appendixes in the back of the book.

- Make decisions about what you can and can't do and live with your decisions.

- Learn to work efficiently when you are working. Don't waste time with needless activity.

$ How to Save Dollars
$ for Family Fun

In this section of the book, we'll be talking about how to save those all-important dollars so that we have finances to invest in family fun. While it's important to have enough money, I'm not sure that having a *lot* of money is any assurance of having the most fun. Recently, someone did a study on a virtually cashless culture and learned that those people were some of the hap-

> God doesn't need money to meet our needs. He does expect us to pay attention and to use our heads about how we use our money.

piest on earth. So whatever money you have, cultivate a thankful attitude and ask God to expand your resources. Don't be afraid to invest money for family fun. It's an investment in your kids that will have huge returns in terms of relationships, hands-on educational value, and exposure to a wider world than their home, school, and church.

Some of the wisest words I ever heard were, "Don't always think in terms of satisfying your needs with money. There may be another way to meet those needs." You see, God doesn't need money to meet our needs. He does expect us to pay attention and to use our heads about how we use our money. So here are some basic rules to get us going in this section.

● Establish the habit of tithing. There is an underlying principle in tithing that God honors. Even those who do not claim faith in God but who tithe to some kind of charitable institution are blessed. There is something about being sure we have our tithe ready to give each week that causes us to evaluate every decision we make about spending money. It doesn't work to tithe just so God will reward us with lots of wealth. We have to tithe because this is what God has asked us to do. Then we have to leave the rest—having enough money to meet our other bills—to God. He will honor our commitment.

● Set your standard of living at a comfortable but not excessive level. Figure out how much you absolutely have to have to be comfortable and all through your life stick to that decision. There is a constant temptation to let that level of supposed needs and comforts creep upward, costing you more and more each year. Of course, if your situation changes, you need to be flexible and adjust accordingly.

● Live life with gratitude. We are so wealthy in comparison to any generation or culture that has ever lived on earth. Even the poorest among us has more than many people in today's third-world cultures. And remember, it isn't how much you have, it is the quality of life that is most important.

● Most of us need a budget, but a budget isn't a thing to be dreaded. It is a plan for spending that assures you can go on a vacation and not dread the bills that follow. It means having the cash to meet a family emergency.

● Look to God for guidance about spending money. God has a plan for every family. He is more interested in what happens to your family and the individuals that make it up than you will ever be. God loves you and wants the best for you. Realize every morning that he has your best interests at heart. He wants your kids to have braces and the best schooling possible. He wants you to have rest and recreation. He wants you to have an adequate diet and good health. God is for you!

- Trust God. In the end, it always comes down to trust. We have to trust God with today, with our future, and with our finances. Most of us don't have any trouble trusting him with eternity. It's today that scares us. But it really doesn't make much sense to trust him with our eternal souls and then lie awake in fear of financial ruin—does it? Search his Word for assurance that he will care for us; then leave the rest to him. God's resources are so much greater than ours that we just don't have the mental capacity to see how he might meet our need.

make a plan for fun

"Whadda ya wanna do?"

"I don't know. Whadda ya wanna do?"

So went the conversation of the buzzards in *The Jungle Book*. I don't remember that they ever decided to do anything at all, except talk about it.

Some families are like that too. "Whadda ya wanna do?"

"I don't know. Whadda ya wanna do?" And so these families often do nothing about having fun together.

As much as possible, involve your whole family in the planning process. When you work together, not only do you come up with great fun-time ideas, you also teach your kids how to do research on a given topic and how to organize an event.

Planning is vital in order to teach children our values through shared experiences. We have to plan to spend time with them. We have to plan the time we spend with them. And we have to plan what values we want them to acquire through the experience. If we fail to plan, other commitments will swallow the time we should be giving to our family. You already know that's true.

Making no plan is a plan in itself—a plan to fail at spending time with the most important people on earth, our family. We need to write "special appointment" across whole days or at least parts of days to be set aside for family activities. Keep these appointments with your family as if they were sacred commitments. They are. Twenty years from now, your kids will not remember what you bought with all that money you made working overtime, but your son will remember the ball game you came to when he hit his first home run. Your daughter will remember your being in the audience when she played her first piano solo. And you will remember too.

Planning for family fun falters when no one steps up to the plate to do it. But in every family, there is usually someone who enjoys figuring out ad-

> **We need to write "special appointment" across whole days or at least parts of days to be set aside for family activities.**

28

ventures for the family. And it may not be the mother or father. It may be one of the older kids.

Where Do I Get Ideas for Fun with Kids?

■ This Book

First of all, this book has been written to give you hundreds of fun ideas that can be adapted to your area and your family. Study it. Keep it on your shelf as reference. Read it and let it inspire you to create your own adventures. Try as I might, I have not captured all the fun things families can do together. Be your own researcher.

■ Libraries

Let's start with the library. Libraries are free, almost every town has one, and they are all filled with wonderful information and amazing tools.

Do you know that you don't even have to put the key in your car's ignition to use the library? A great deal of library information is accessible online. Learn to use your online library.

From the library you can get free videos and DVDs, music CDs, books on tape and CD, magazines, and, of course, books. Go online to the library catalog, where you can order what you want your family to view, read, or hear. Then all you need to do is make a quick trip to the library to pick up the material when it comes in. You're all set for an evening of fun at home, and it's all free. Oh, and don't forget the popcorn.

Kids can get help with homework at some libraries through homework centers right at the library, or kids can go online to gather information and get the help they need. Check out what is available in your town.

Libraries are filled with regional publications: books, pamphlets, maps, videos on specific places, newspapers, and lots more material. Go to the travel section of your library. If your planned event will take you beyond your region, you should spend time investigating this section. In the travel section, you'll find ideas for travel for all budgets—from backpacking to the most elegant hotels and restaurants. Most libraries also have a table where there are pamphlets and flyers for upcoming local events.

The library is a treasure house of valuable information and ideas for your family's fun adventures. Take your whole family to the library on a discovery trip. Or take them there for a story hour or puppet show. Your taxes help to keep the doors of the library open, so take advantage of all the information it offers. You've already paid for it.

■ Newspapers

Another wonderful source of information for family adventures is the newspaper. Metropolitan newspapers have a calendar section that comes out periodically (once a month or once a week). To save both money and time, you don't have to take a paper every day. Just figure out what day gives you that all-important calendar page and buy that day's paper. In the calendar section, you will find theater showings and plays, exhibitions in museums, concerts, sporting events, festivals, and fairs.

Not only does the calendar section of the paper provide ideas, so does the travel page. We often think the travel page is just for foreign travel, but that's not true. Travel pages carry articles about local events, short trips, camping areas, music events, and, once again, museum ideas. For example, our local newspaper recently had a piece on an Oz Museum in the town of Wamego, Kansas. There the visitor will find two thousand pieces of memorabilia from the *Wizard of Oz* movie and books. The museum also has pictures of the farm from which Dorothy flew off to Oz in a tornado. I don't live anywhere near Kansas, but if I were traveling that way, I'd try to find this little museum and give my family a memorable experience.

There are more ideas for family fun in one newspaper than you could find time to do in six months.

31

■ Chamber of Commerce

The local Chamber of Commerce also has schedules of events happening in your city. Check it out online. I find that some sites are better maintained than others. You'll have to take a look to see how current your local site is. Even though you might not be visiting the West Coast anytime soon, to see a really great Chamber of Commerce website, check out Santa Barbara's. They have a very up-to-date listing of information.

■ Bookstores

Bookstores are a family's best friend.

Bookstores are a family's best friend. Bookstores have story hours, demonstrations, and, of course, books, CDs, and DVDs for sale. When you are visiting a bookstore, invest in a couple of regional books that relate to what your family likes to do. It could be biking trips, hikes, architectural walks through a city, places to view wildlife, or garden tours.

■ Regional Magazines

Regional magazines are yet another source of ideas for family fun. Every major city has a magazine, and regions of the country also have magazines just filled with ideas for family fun. If you are planning a major trip to an area, subscribe to a magazine for a year. You'll find information about the history of the area, bed and breakfast places, hotels, tours, amusement parks, sporting events and their calendars, and lots of other useful information.

■ *Yellow Pages*

Gather ideas from your local yellow pages, either online or from the telephone book. (Some online sites charge for their services, but a great nationwide site that is free is www .whiteyellowpages.com.) Just browsing the yellow pages can give you loads of ideas for places to go and things to do. The phone book also has dollars-off coupons for some events.

If you are using the online version, put in a category for your search, for example, "entertainment." To show you how it works, let's take a look at the Los Angeles site. There are:

- Aircraft sightseeing tours.
- Bicycle tours.
- Marine vessels and tours.
- Raft trips and tours.
- Scuba sightseeing tours (would be great for teens).
- More than a hundred sightseeing tours and attractions.

When you go to just one of those sites—say, bicycle tours—
you will find links to other sites of interest on the same subject.
Some examples follow.

- Bicycle tours worldwide (www.backroads.com): "Over
  20 years of experience offering variety in bicycling, walking, and multisport vacations featuring inspiring routes,
  fine accommodations, cuisine, and great leaders."

- Ciclismo Classico bicycle tours (www.ciclismoclassico
  .com): "Bicycle tours in Italy and New England. Active, educational and fun bicycle tours for all ages and abilities."

- Supported bicycle tours in eight countries (www
  .experienceplus.com): "Explore Europe or Costa Rica
  by bike on 30 tours in eight countries. Visit the family
  farm in Italy on our family or single tour. Bicycling
  and eating with Experienceplus
  since 1971."

- And finally we get to the
  Los Angeles company
  we came to view: LA
  Bike Tours—Toll-
  free 888-775-2453,
  323-466-5890, or
  www.hollywood
  probicycles.com/labt
  .html (in case you're interested in pursuing this
  one).

Friends

One of the best places to get ideas for family fun is from your friends and the parents of your kids' friends. Where do they take their kids to eat? What is their kids' favorite event in your area? Where do they picnic? Where do they camp? Talk to busy people because they are the ones who are out there doing things.

Curiosity

Don't overlook your kid's curiosity as a source of ideas for things to do. "Hey, Dad, how does milk get to our stores?"

"Well, I could tell you, but let me see if I can arrange a tour of a dairy, and then you can see for yourself."

The Internet

Learn to use the Internet as a tool for finding family fun. A great Internet site is www.thingstodo.com. Or just go to Google and put in the words "things to do." You'll have a dozen sites come up that are full of useful information. You can access any area of the country, so if you are traveling to Minnesota or Alabama, you can find out what's happening there and when. For fun, give it a try.

Access local information by going to a major search site and

35

typing in your county's name. This will bring up very detailed information about events in your county. Or type "children and family entertainment" into your search engine. On Google, I found twenty-two pages of listings for family entertainment. The site www.smartpages.com is yet another that's loaded with information on family entertainment. If you are researching "museums," you'll not only find listings of museums in your area, but phone numbers, hours, free days, website information, driving directions with a map you can print, and the opportunity to search for other places nearby, such as a restaurant or other entertainment opportunities.

After all that searching on the Internet, you may want to print out hard copies of the fun ideas you find rather than trying to remember what website held all that wonderful info. Keep those printed sheets in your paper file for quick access.

■ Travel Companies

Write for free travel information or let your kids clip and mail the coupons for free travel information found in magazines. Not only will they be helping you find family fun ideas, they will enjoy getting mail on a regular basis as the information comes in. Then drop the brochures and travel pamphlets in your file.

■ Newspapers

Train yourself to watch for ideas and then clip them out on the spot and put them in a paper file (described below). There may be someone in your house who asks, "Who cut a hole in the paper?" However, if you don't cut out the articles when you first see them, chances are someone will throw out the paper and the information will be lost.

Organizing All That Information

The secret to having plenty of information ready when you want to pursue a family adventure is to gather information before you need it. But if you've already tried any of the suggestions above, you probably have more information than you know what to do with. Now you have another problem: how to keep track of it. You need to create a system.

> The secret to having plenty of information ready when you want to pursue a family adventure is to gather information before you need it.

■ A Paper File

The best way to organize newspaper and magazine clippings is in a paper file. A filing system doesn't have to be elaborate, but it is essential to have some way to keep accessible the information you've collected. Make yourself a simple file by getting a cardboard or an inexpensive plastic box sold at any office-supply store. Buy some file folders. If you like to color code your ideas and file folders (blue is for water adventures, red for big-city adventures), buy colored folders or use colored tabs.

A Computer File

Perhaps for you, a folder on your computer's desktop might be the best way for you to access the information you find online. Just find something that works for keeping track so that you don't have to research again.

For Either Method of Filing

There are several methods for filing information.

- Filing by *location* simply means creating folders with country, state, county, or city names of interest. Drop all those clipped items into the file so that when Kalamazoo is on your route, you'll have ideas for what to see there.

- Filing by *interests* is done first of all by identifying your family's interests. If your family loves to watch hang gliders, gather every piece of information you can find on places where hang gliders practice their sport. File the information. If your family loves ice cream, file everything you can find about ice cream. Then when you are traveling to a new location, you just might have a great ice-cream experience for them.

38

- Or you can file by *subject*. Here are some possible headings and ideas about what could go into those folders.

Agriculture

- Dairy farms: Most will give a tour if you call ahead.

- Farms: Pick your own fruits and vegetables. Watch for ads and roadside signs.

- Horse ranches: Visit the blacksmith shop.

- Research farms: Here you'll learn of the latest discoveries.

Arts

- Ballet: Expose your children to ballet. *The Nutcracker* is a delightful story and is performed annually at Christmastime in many cities.

- Opera: This can be fun for the whole family, but to get anything out of the experience, everyone has to know the story before the singing begins.

- Art galleries: Visit permanent exhibits and keep watch for traveling exhibits.

- Outdoor concerts: These are performed in many places throughout the summer season.

- Cinema: Pick out a good movie. Some theaters have special showings for kids.

- Laserium (to see a laser show) or IMAX.

Communications

- Television stations: Watch for times when stations are open for visits.

- Radio stations: Let your children see the announcers and disc jockeys they hear on the air.

- Telephone companies: Tour a facility and learn about modern communication systems.

Cultural

- Folk festivals: These are plentiful in most states throughout the summer months.

- Ethnic food fairs: Watch for announcements in the newspaper and on television. Then when you get there, make the rounds and try everything.

- Native American events: You'll find these in many states.

Drama

- Seasonal events: In many cities, *A Christmas Carol* is performed during the holiday season.

40

- Theatrical performances in city parks: Check the newspaper for these. They are family oriented and can be a lot of fun.

- Community theaters: Some may be children's theater.

- Shakespearean festival: Read the story synopsis before going.

Government

- Government buildings: Many have tours. Visit your state's capitol or tour your city hall.

- Courts of law: These are interesting places to visit and in most cases can be toured when court is not in session.

- Police stations and fire stations: Call to find out their schedules for tours.

History

- Sunday paper: History seems to be a favorite topic for newspaper writers. Clip interesting articles and save them in your file.

- State parks: State parks are often located at historical sites. Write to your state park system or search online.

41

- Old homes and buildings: Tours are offered annually by many societies. Watch for their announcements in the newspaper.

- Regional publications: *Sunset* magazine in the West and *Southern Living* magazine in the South often include information about historical events and places. Read the library issues and photocopy the articles that interest you.

Industry

- Candy factories: Guests are usually welcome. You'll have to make arrangements to tour the larger ones. Most have a seconds (rejects) shop that will make candy factories a favorite stop for your family.

- Pulp mills: See how paper is made.

- Woolen and cotton mills: Learn about making fabrics.

Nature

- Botany: File information on formal gardens and arboretums where you can see regional plants.

- Marine life: If you live near the ocean or a lake, this may be of interest.

- Wild animals: Keep information on zoos and game farms.

- Birds: Some people make a lifelong hobby of watching birds.

- Astronomy: Local planetariums are worth a visit.

Science

- Science centers and museums: There are many events geared for children and young people.

- Universities: Science programs are often open to the public. Call the university's office, make notes of its programs, and file them.

Transportation

- Trains: Collect schedules to the nearest towns. If your children have never ridden on a train, plan to do it. Just go a short distance and return home on the next train.

- Model trains: There are many model-train clubs around the country. It's amazing to see the amount of time and energy adults put into playing with trains.

- Airplanes: Airports and air museums are fascinating places for kids.

- Trucks: Visit a local dispatcher at a truck terminal and

43

watch how truckers handle the big rigs. Maybe you'll be able to ride in the cab of a truck.

- Hot air balloon ride.
- Helicopter ride.
- Boat rides: in a ferry or sailboat; rowing or canoeing; on a whale-watching or sightseeing cruise.
- Bus tour: Most cities have a tour bus. The one in Seattle is in an amphibious army vehicle. First you drive through the city, and at the end, you splash into the water of the sound.

Mapping Out a Specific Plan

Let's suppose you found something of interest in your file—an adventure you want to pursue. Now it's time to plan the event. The following checklist will help you think through every part of your event.

____ Where are we going?

____ Who's going on this adventure?

____ How far away is it?

____ What time do we need to leave?

____ What kind of clothing is appropriate?

____ Do we need to take food or drinks?

____ How much money will we need?

____ Is there enough gas in the car?

____ If it is a ticketed event, have we bought the tickets?

____ Where are the tickets?

____ How long will we be gone?

____ Do we need pet care?

____ Will we need to eat a meal on the road or in a restaurant?

____ What favorite toy, blanket, or pillow should be taken so there are no tears later because it is missing?

____ Have we done our research on the place or event? (Take this book or one with the research information along for reference en route or at the event.)

Once you've really thought through the entire excursion and taken all the necessary actions, you should be ready to launch.

When Plans Go Wrong

Not all plans work out as expected. The best plans do go awry sometimes. You can't do much about that, except possibly have an alternative plan. The alternative will not be your first choice, and your family may not be quite as excited about this second adventure, but having an alternative plan will help take

Be flexible, be adventurous, and be prepared to re-group and head in another direction when the bottom falls out of your first idea.

the sting out of losing the first adventure. Who knows, that second adventure might turn out to be more fun than the first would have been. Be flexible, be adventurous, and be prepared to regroup and head in another direction when the bottom falls out of your first idea.

I've said it before, but it bears repeating: the most important thing we can do is spend time with our kids, whether it's adventure one or adventure two. We can't teach our values to our children unless we spend quality time with them, and quality time must be planned. So block out time on the calendar, gather the information and do the research so that you know what to expect, file the research information where you can find it, bring your children into your planning process, and if the plan fails, regroup and do something else.

If we take the time to plan our adventures carefully, we will reap the full benefit of shared experiences with our children, and they will learn what we treasure and value in our lives.

So are you ready for the adventure of having fun as a family? *Then let's go!*

part II

start from
home base

nesting

Family Night in Your Nest

After 9-11, people began to draw together at home in a way that had not been seen for a long time. The word "nesting" began to show up on television and in magazines and newspapers. The family home is a place where we can draw together those we love and where there is comparative safety from the complex world we live in. And the family nest can be not only a place of safety, but a place for fun and learning. So here we're going to look at an old-fashioned idea: family night.

Some old-fashioned ideas are good ones and are worthy of being preserved. It's interesting to think back to the time when most people lived on farms. During the daytime, children and parents worked side by side in the fields and with the family's animals. After a day of working together, most families gathered for dinner. They'd sit around in the kitchen or on the porch for a while, and then they would fall into bed exhausted. In that culture, *every* day was family day, and *every* night was family night. But such togetherness is not the case today.

Today, when we go our separate ways for most of the day, family nights have to be planned, or it might be weeks before everyone in the family is in the same room for a sustained period of time. And, once again, there is no way to teach your children what matters to you as a family—your values and beliefs—without spending time with them.

Talk in your planning time about what should happen at your family night. Why are we doing this? Help your children come to the conclusion that we are doing it to have fun together and to strengthen our family in every way, including spiritually.

> There is no way to teach your children what matters to you as a family—your values and beliefs—without spending time with them.

Family nights need rules. Get everyone together for a planning time in which you draw up your rules. Children buy into rules more quickly if they are the ones who set them up, so give them the opportunity. In case you need some help, here are some basic rules for family night.

■ *Rules*

- *We will observe one night each week as family night.* It's best if family night is the same night every week. Teach family members to plan ahead and not to schedule anything else on this night. Sometimes events over which you have no control happen on the same night as your family night. Not a problem. Just pick another night in the same week. However you handle your situation, remember to regard the time together as a sacred commitment. It truly is, you know.

- *Each family member will take a turn at planning the night's activities* (more about activities later). Everybody, from the youngest to the oldest, has to take a turn. Little ones will probably need assistance in their planning from the big people in the family. Even so, it is important that little ones have a turn too. If a family member absolutely cannot fulfill his obligation, he can switch nights with another family member, but he cannot completely get out of being in charge of a family night. He must fulfill his obligations to the family unit.

● *Everyone must participate in the planned activities.* Mom and Dad must protect the self-esteem of the planner and enforce the idea of total family participation. Building up the self-esteem of the people who live in your house is a very important part of parenting.

● *Everyone must show respect for the plan and the planner.* Ban criticism that comes out in a negative way, such as, "This is dumb." Everybody will have a turn at respecting other people's ideas and having their own ideas respected.

■ *Scripture Reading and Prayer*

Scripture reading and prayer should be a part of almost every family night. (The exception might be when family night includes an outing.) The Scripture can be from a Bible storybook or a modern-English translation, so that children can understand and enjoy what they are reading and hearing. Prayer can be conversational or written down or silent. God will take delight in hearing your family reading his Word and praying together. When they are older, some children may stray from their Christian beliefs and practices, but they will never forget the values and spiritual insights they have learned in your family nights.

How to Plan Family Nights

Get your kids involved in planning your family nights. Do the things they love but make sure to include teachable moments.

Here is a list of suggestions. Feel free to add your own ideas to the list.

- *Story night*: Story night can be a night when family members make up a story ahead of time to tell. They can write it out, dramatize it, or depict it with drawings. Or story night can be when Mom or Dad tell stories about "the olden days when you were little." Or it can be stories your parents told you when you were little. Tell funny stories. Tell sad stories. Tell stories you've heard about other families. Just tell stories. These are cultural treasures no one can ever take from your children.

- *Film night*: This might be an easy family night event when everyone is too tired to plan something. But even here, there needs to be *some* planning. You, as parents, need to do your homework on the films, videos, and DVDs your family will be watching. Be very careful about the rating. The ratings are not always trustworthy. Some G-rated films have more questionable material than some PG-13 films. Choose something that teaches a positive value. There are many websites that will help you in your selection. Here are two: http://www.aap.org/family/ratingsgame.htm and http://www.dove.org/default.asp.

- *Celebrate-a-special-day night*: Celebrate someone's birthday—anyone's birthday. It doesn't have to be a member of your family. Celebrate the birthday of one of our presidents or a well-known person or a pet. Or look online to find out what happened on this day in history. It could be the anniversary of Lindbergh's arrival in Paris, or the day the United States beat the Soviets in Olympic hockey, or the last day of summer, or Valentine's Day. It doesn't really matter what it is—celebrate. Get paper hats or a piñata, tint the food green, blow up balloons and tie them all around the house. Do you get the idea? It doesn't matter what it is you celebrate. What matters is who you are with . . . your family. And it matters that your family has fun as you build memories together. (See lots more ideas for family celebrations in chapter 6.)

- *Make-a-project night*: There are literally hundreds, perhaps thousands, of fun, simple, and inexpensive projects you can do with your children. One website, http://family fun.go.com/crafts, will give you more ideas than you can do in a year. And there are hundreds of such sites. Make-a-project night can run the gamut of complexity. Maybe your make-it project is cookies for a holiday, or it could be a build-a-sundae project where you provide ice cream and an array of toppings and syrups and let everyone build their own sundae. Fun and yummy! Or build something out of cardboard boxes, such as the skyscraper suggested on the website above. You could make your own greeting cards by stamping paper folded to card size. Or make your own wrapping paper by stamping butcher paper or brown wrapping paper that comes in rolls. Use either ready-made commercial stamps or make your own stamps from sliced fruit or carved potatoes. Perhaps you can gather moss and sticks to make gift baskets for grandparents or aunts and uncles. Fill them with small flowering plants. As I said, there are a multitude of ideas for things to make with your kids. If you don't need to be careful about spending money (and this book advocates saving money as much as you can), buy some kind of kit that will provide an evening's activity for your family to work on together. It's a good investment in family life.

- *Reading night*: We're going to talk a lot more about reading later in this chapter, but for planning family night activities, just incorporate reading as one of the activities. You could read picture books and short stories, or you could have an ongoing story that you read a little from each time you have a family night. Teachers use this idea in their classrooms, and kids stop moving and sit entranced as the teacher reads. They don't seem to have any trouble taking up the thread of the story from week to week.

● *Drama night*: Drama done as a family can be a hilarious event. When I was a child and our extended family visited, we often did dramas together. They were made up on the spot and were absolutely hilarious. Years later, I still remember some of the dramas we acted out. But even if I didn't remember them, I remember how much fun we all had together. You can act out Bible stories, stories from books you have read together, historical stories, or stories you make up. The key to the fun is letting everyone participate and having items on hand from which to make costumes. I used to keep a trunk full of old clothes, shawls, wigs, hats, beads, and anything else that could be turned into a costume. I picked up these items at garage sales and in thrift stores, or they were recycled from my own closet. I saved every school costume and added it to the trunk. By the way, you might want to draw the shades so you don't have to explain to the neighbors why you are running around in your house wearing bathrobes and crowns.

- *Go-someplace-special night*: These family nights are very special. The planner for the evening's event thinks up something unique for the whole family to do. It might be a visit to a planetarium or just a trip outside to view the stars, moon, and planets with a borrowed telescope. It might be to go see a play in the park or to go backstage at the circus. What happens in your area that is unique? Search it out. Is it a nighttime parade, a concert under the stars, or a visit to a bookstore? Always end your night out with an edible treat—it heightens the experience. Have sundaes at a local restaurant or caramel popcorn and pretzels at the mall. Make this night very special and help your planner by offering finances for the evening.

- *Fun night*: This is an at-home night when the family plays games together. It can be balloon volleyball in the

Wonderful programs of charity have grown from kids who saw a need and didn't know it couldn't be done. They just went ahead and did it.

living room or board games at the dining-room table. You could even ask friends in to share your fun time.

● *Others night*: This is a night that focuses on the less fortunate. If it is appropriate, take your children to see how some people in your city live. Go to a mission or other shelter. Talk with your kids about what Jesus said about helping the poor. Figure out a way your family can make a difference. Wonderful programs of charity have grown from kids who saw a need and didn't know it couldn't be done. They just went ahead and did it.

● *Bible night*: Focus on God's Word on this night. Read Bible passages and act them out. Or let the children draw pictures that depict the story. Or get magazines and tear out pictures and paste them on a board as a kind of collage of the story that was read. If your kids are school-age and can read well, have an old-fashioned sword drill in which you give a Scripture reference and the kids look it up. First one to find it reads the reference and gets a point. Give some kind of reward to the winner.

● *Show-and-tell night*: Let each
child show something he
or she has and tell why
it is special. It can be a
hobby, a collection, a
riddle, or a joke. Par-
ents might drag out
objects and pictures
of when the kids were
younger. Ever compare
the first shoes your baby
wore with the size elevens your
teenager now sports? It's amazing to say the least.

● *Music night*: You don't have to be a musician to have a
music night. Put in a CD with a lively beat and march
around the house. Or play a classical piece and have the
kids draw a picture of what the music tells them. Form
a band using kitchen implements for instruments and
bang away with joy. Even the Bible says to make a joy-
ful noise to the Lord. If your children are taking music
lessons, from time to time let them play for each other,
and be sure due praise is given by all the family members
for the achievement the performer has earned.

● *Surprise night*: This can be anything the whole family
can participate in. You can go to a new animated film
together, but don't tell the kids where they are going till
they get there. Or you could pack their bags and go off
for the night to a hotel where they can swim and play
video games. The end of the destination also may be a

grandparent's house in another city. Of course, grandma and grandpa have to be in on the secret. Just surprise your kids with good things.

● *Talk-it-over night* (family council): This family night is not the most fun, but it may be the most important. It is a scheduled time when the whole family can sit down, make decisions together, air differences, coordinate schedules, and do a host of other things. Family council is a great time for setting goals for your family. Talk about vacations you might want to take, events you might want to be a part of, places you want to go, family financial goals, and educational goals. Every family needs a family council. It avoids sweeping little problems under the rug until one day there is a huge problem at your house that no one ever wanted to talk about. Family council keeps the lines of communication open. You should be ready to take some criticism from your children for words you have said, actions you have taken, and attitudes you have displayed.

Home, the Best Place for Reading and Watching Television Together

■ *Why Spend Time Reading Together?*

If you glean only one thing from this book, make it this: *Reading is the most important gift you can give your child.*

Want to grow a great reader? Want to build a close relationship with your kids? Want to see them excel in their studies? Then read to them.

A number of years ago, an expensive government study concluded that the best way to grow an early reader was not to put your children in a Head Start or Montessori program, nor to buy them some expensive reading program. The best way to grow an early reader and help your child love reading is to take him on your lap as soon as he can sit up and read to him. The combination of a parent's arms about him, Mom's or Dad's words in his ear, and the shared experience with a book is the very best approach to growing kids who can read.

Reading is the most important gift you can give your child.

A child who is familiar with books *has* a head start on life. From books it is possible to learn about places you may never be able to go. You can become familiar with people you may never meet. With books you can step backward through time and understand the peoples of past centuries. You can learn to make houses and gardens. You can learn to repair a car, design a gar-

61

ment, or teach a dog to obey. You can learn about the mysteries of space and the complex world of the cell. There is a book for every idea that enters your head. And it is through a particular book, the Bible, that you and your child will learn the path to eternal life.

As a parent, I always felt that if my kids read and understood what they were reading, they would be able to figure out most anything life threw at them. They would be able to express themselves both on paper and verbally, because they would understand how words best fit together. They could go on to be teachers, lawyers, writers, preachers, and a host of other professions that depend on verbal skills. And if they chose manual work, they would be able to communicate with others, both customers and employers, in clear and easy-to-understand language.

Reading aloud provides a family with a forum for all kinds of discussion—first about the story, and then about the values of the people in the story, and later about your family's values on the same subject.

You can deliberately select a book that addresses a value you want to emphasize to your family. For example, if you have a problem with a child who lies, read a book that tells what happened to the main character when he told lies. Then discuss the story. If we are to communicate our value system to our children, we have to be able to talk with them. An excellent way to begin communicating is through reading aloud together and then discussing what you've read.

Don't view reading to a child as one more thing on your "to do" list. It doesn't have to be drudgery. Be a little bit selfish and reread some of your favorite stories from your childhood. Or do as I did and read many of the stories and books I had missed as a child. Read what all of you will enjoy. Just make the commitment to read to your kids. The time I invested in reading to my children is an investment that keeps paying all of us back.

When Shall We Read?

Read anytime and anyplace.

- Keep a book handy for times when you must wait for others. Kids hate waiting and can become unbearable. A good story helps to speed the time for all of you.

- Read in the car when your family is traveling.

- Read to your children for ten or fifteen minutes just before their bedtime. Reading has a tremendously soothing effect.

● Set aside a special time each week for reading together as a family. Sunday afternoons or Saturday evenings are often times when little else is scheduled.

● Vacation can be a time for reading something very special. Perhaps you'll find, as my family did, that reading one book together generated the desire to read another . . . and another. We saved some of the longer books for vacation, when we would have an extended period of time to read.

● Remember that having a book with you, ready to be read, is better than many shelves of unread books at home.

■ What Shall We Read?

First of all, get a good Bible storybook. What a wonderful time to be living in, because there are dozens of Bible storybooks with wonderful art. Choosing one for your family may just be a matter of preference. You could make one of your family night outings to a bookstore to select a Bible storybook. There is something very quieting and comforting when a child learns that God is always there, watching, protecting, and loving. There is assurance for the parent who learns that God is pro-family, able to deliver, and in control of all things. Families who read Bible stories together will grow in their inner beings.

When reading aloud from the Bible itself, choose a Bible version with language very much like that used in the everyday world of kids.

Let me say just a word about reading fantasy. Some parents don't know what to think of it. Well, there's good fantasy, and there's not-so-good fantasy. Terrifying, occultish, belligerent fantasy is not for the Christian family. But fantasy that expands the mind to new possibilities causes the readers and listeners to think more broadly and more creatively than they have in the past.

Michael Gurian, writer of many books on the subject of boys' brain development, says that story, particularly story that involves the inclusion of an archetypal character, perhaps even in the realm of fantasy, can be one of the best ways to reach a boy's thinking and value system. He suggests we search for stories that have no easy answers. These are the stories of heroes, warriors, angels, prophets, kings, giants, and so forth. As boys hear stories, through asking and having their questions answered, they can be guided to embrace courage, compassion, and goals that are filled with spiritual, moral, and value-laden content. In our culture, information comes to our children through stereotypes—pop stars, sports figures, and others. Our children get information from these sources, but they do not get wisdom. Wisdom comes from thinking about the struggle of good and evil, both in imaginary stories and in biblical stories. Gurian concludes that preaching to a boy is rarely effective, but showing him through story works much better.[*]

Some of the great classics of children's literature, such as The Chronicles of Narnia by C. S. Lewis and The Lord of the Rings by J.R.R. Tolkien, are fantasy tales with powerful

*Gurian, Michael, and Jeremy P. Tarcher, *The Wonder of Boys*. New York: Putnam, 1996.

messages of the struggle between good and evil. Share these wonderful stories with your children. It will be good for your entire family.

Family reading should encompass a broad spectrum of literature. It should include history (told at a child's level), adventure stories, poetry, geography, humorous pieces, and animal stories. There should be picture books, including pop-up or board books, rhyming books, easy-reader books, and books written in words that paint glowing landscapes for the mind.

■ *Other Guidelines to Help You Choose Reading Material*

● *Choose appropriate age-level books.* Children's books now come with an age level or reading level printed on them. Look for it. If it is not there, bookstores and libraries have help-desk personnel to assist you. There are also books available that give reading lists for certain age levels. I still like Gladys Hunt's book *Honey for a Child's Heart,* first published years ago by Zondervan. There is a wonderful reading list in the back of her book.

● *Find books that appeal to the entire family.* The biggest challenge for families with children whose ages are spread out is finding books that appeal to all the age levels represented in a family. Talk to your librarian for ideas on what has broad appeal to all age groups. If you find the book you start to read is too difficult for the younger members of the family or too inane for the adults, don't consider your reading program a failure. Put the book aside and choose something more to the tastes of everyone.

● *Books do not have to be geared to the youngest family member.* Although the youngest child may not get the meaning of every word spoken or the wonderful nuances of the language, she will get enough of the story to enjoy it. If words need to be explained so the meaning of the story is not lost, stop and explain them. It's a great way to build vocabulary.

Websites to Encourage Family Reading

There are a number of websites that provide help for parents who want their children to be readers. Although there are hundreds of sites, here are a few.

● Reading Families Program, A Family Literacy Initiative: http://gargoyle.arcadia.edu/readingfamilies/

● Scott Foresman: http://www.sfreading.com/families .html

- San Jose Public Libraries and State University: http://www.sjlibrary.org/services/literacy/par/ffl.htm

- A Bridge to Reading: http://www.mpt.org/learning works/bridgetoreading/moreinfo/index.cfm

Make Your Television a Tool for Growth

Years ago when I first wrote about television and family life, I saw television as a potential problem area. Well, that was nothing compared with the problem we have now. With an ongoing discussion about how much profanity will be allowed on television, sexual explicitness (both heterosexual and homosexual), crass commercialism, and lousy programming, we have an even bigger problem. And it's *your* problem if you are raising kids. Some have called television "the Third Parent." Children as young as eighteen months are parked in front of a television as a babysitter. By the time kids graduate from high school, they could well have seen 18,000 hours of television. That compares to 13,000 spent in the classroom. And by the time they reach the sixth grade, they could have seen 100,000 acts of violence and 8,000 murders. Oh, by the way, they see about 20,000 commercials each year—20,000 commercials that will only increase their consumer appetite.

I'm not one who thinks you should get rid of your television. That's way too easy. The neighbors have a television your kids can watch without your being there. More than that, our entire culture is being impacted by television, and even if you sell your set, your kids' world—the clothes they wear, the food they eat, the slang they use—comes directly or indirectly from television. So to be in control of how your kids are being impacted by television, you have to be there with them watching and

controlling what they see. You are the parent, and you must protect those God has entrusted to you. Guess what? The kids will go along with your decisions when you make them, but you may be the biggest problem. You too may have to give up viewing some of your favorite shows in order to set a good example for your children.

Have I lost my reading audience? I hope not. We're not going to focus on the "should nots." You already know them. Let's focus on how to make television a tool for good in your family.

● *Decide as a family how much time you will spend watching television.* Did you know that children watch television an average of twenty-four hours a week? That's three-and-a-half hours each day that they are not reading, playing outdoors, learning a craft or how to make something, or even relating to other kids? Did you know that a huge percentage of children have television sets in their rooms? How is a child going to learn relational skills while shut up in his room alone? So have the talk with your kids. How much television is reasonable for your family?

● *Decide what you will watch . . . ahead of time.* Invest in a television guide either in magazine form or from the Sunday paper and spend part of Sunday afternoon going over it searching for good programming that will actually add to your family's life. Highlight those programs and decide to either watch them at actual viewing times or tape them for viewing at more convenient times. (Sometimes some of the best movies come on in the middle of the night.) Select television programs that reflect your family's values, such as honesty; consideration for others; caring; having good, wholesome fun not at another's expense; and so on.

● *Set an example for your kids by limiting the amount of time you watch television.* Have a time each day that is set aside for reading and talking. Have lots of books in your home. There is no way a kid can get interested in reading if he never sees a book in your home. (See the "How to Save $ for Family Fun" section for ideas of where to get books.)

● *Watch television with your kids.* You will be amazed at what they are seeing even when watching cartoons. Watching with your kids not only monitors what they are seeing, but allows you to interpret what they see in

70

terms of your family's values. You can be watching the world's safest sitcom when suddenly one of the characters says or does something that does not line up with your family value system.

- *Include television viewing that can act as a springboard for learning.* Channels such as National Geographic or The Learning Channel sometimes have programming that is wonderful in its educational value. Use this kind of programming to help your kids learn. For example, you watch a program on seals and their amazing water acrobatics. After the program is over, shut off the television, go to the computer or to books you have brought from the library, and sit down together and talk about the program. Learn together. It's an awesome experience.

- *Keep a viewing diary.* If you needed to lose weight, the first thing a diet program will ask you to do is to keep a food diary so that you can see what's going into your mouth. Keeping a television diary will help your family know just how much and what kind of programs you are watching. Here's a simple chart to help you set up a viewing diary.

71

Day	Time	Program	Who Watched	How Long
2/10	6 p.m.	Name of program	Sam and Lisa	1 hour
2/10	8 p.m.	Sports	Dad and Sam	2 ½ hours
2/10	11 p.m.	News	Mom and Dad	½ hour

● *Interpret what your kids see.* Help them understand that sitcoms, cartoons, or anything other than real-life television is fantasy—made up. Help them see through the bias of the scriptwriters. Help them understand that violence hurts, and sometimes that hurt ends in death, and there is no coming back from death as actors do. Show them that television relies on celebrities to sell products and that much of the programming is about selling something.

● *If you have a V-chip, activate it.* All new televisions come with a V-chip. The V-chip reads information encoded in the rated program and blocks programs from the set based upon the rating selected by the parent. Many parents who have V-chips in their televisions have never activated them. Perhaps they don't know how, or perhaps they don't think the V-chip is of any value. It is, and you should. For more information, here are a couple of websites to help you. Listed on www.ksee24 .com are the ratings to help you decide which setting is appropriate for your child. Another informative site is http://www.cce.cornell.edu/oneida/cce/family living/parentingpages/pp14.htm. Even when you have activated the V-chip, do not rely on it as a substitute parent. Be there for your kids when they are viewing television.

- *Begin to teach media literacy by studying the plots, predicting the endings, and learning how story is put together.* This may be better accomplished by using your television set in combination with a DVD player. Many newer DVDs have extra material that teaches how the story became a movie from the screenwriter's perspective, how certain shots were filmed, and how the actors interpreted the story. This is very interesting and would be great for older kids.

⧖ How to Find Time for Family Fun

- Plan your chores to have more time for family fun at home. Good planning and organization in a home gives stability and a sense of peace to the family. Little children thrive on order and routine. Good organization of your home and chores also frees you to take some time off and enjoy yourself because you know everything will be taken care of in due time. You don't have to always be thinking, "I should be doing the bills . . . or the dishes . . . or mowing the lawn."
- Plan your chores so that you have a large chunk of time when you can do some serious cleaning. This is more than a daily cleanup but less than a major house

cleaning. A weekend blitz works because everyone can help, or you can use two or three hours set aside during the week. When those big tasks are finished, you'll feel more free to go play.

- Try to keep to whatever schedule you set up for yourself. This will keep you from getting so far behind that you have to work overtime to get caught up.

- Keep track of what needs to be done and when. Make a list and post it somewhere obvious if you need to be reminded to do these things. Teach your kids to take care of their own area as soon as possible. Maybe the beds will have lumps after they are made—that's fine. Who cares? Kids should be taught to pick up after themselves as soon as they learn how to leave things lying around. Make a game of it to get them involved.

- Keep a list of household chores and do the dailies first.

a. Make beds.

b. Wipe down the bathrooms with a towel headed for the laundry.

c. Pick up clothes, toys, newspapers, etc.

d. Wash dishes or put them in the dishwasher.

e. Sweep or dust the floors.

f. Start a load of laundry if needed.

- Keep a weekly list of household chores. Here are
some ideas to get you
started making your
list.

    a. Monday—Laun-
    dry (if you only do
    it once a week)

    b. Tuesday—Clean re-
    frigerator and make a
    shopping list at the same
    time

    c. Wednesday—Food shopping and errands

    d. Thursday—House cleaning

    e. Friday—Baking for weekend

    f. Saturday—Play time

    g. Sunday—Church and friends

- Keep a monthly list of household chores. Here's some
ideas to get you started making your list.

    a. January—Take advantage of inventory sales and
    white sales

    b. February—Plan a Valentine's party

    c. March—Think ahead and plan summer vacation

    d. April—Make sure taxes are taken care of by the
    fifteenth

e. May—Send graduation cards

f. June—Vacation? Weddings? Anniversaries?

g. July—Family celebrations, vacations, camp for kids

h. August—Purchase school supplies and clothes

i. September—Get yard and home ready for winter months; make travel plans for holidays

j. October—Plan a harvest celebration

k. November—Plan Thanksgiving dinner and invite guests

l. December—Plan year-end finances and giving; plan Christmas dinner

● Keep track of information you use often and keep it in one place, such as

a. Emergency numbers

b. Names, addresses, and telephone numbers

c. Birthdays and anniversaries

d. Sizes and preferences of all family members

e. Service dates for household appliances and car repair

f. Medical and dental records for all family members

g. Veterinarian phone number, emergency pet numbers, and pet records

h. Phone numbers of favorite places

i. Packing list

j. Shopping list

- Group chores of a similar kind—like shopping and other errands—and do them all at once.
- Simplify your lifestyle.
  a. Get rid of clutter—knickknacks, extra sporting equipment, hobbies no one is doing anymore, school papers, newspapers, mail, junk.

  b. Get rid of houseplants and instead buy cut flowers for yourself once in a while.

  c. Ask about every object you pick up, "Do we really need this?"

  d. Clean out closets and get rid of everything not worn in a year.

  e. Cut down on the number of toys your child has. Encourage her to give toys to the less fortunate.
- Deal with incoming papers.
  a. Drop junk mail straight into the garbage can. It's all right to throw away unopened junk mail.

  b. Put bills in a specific place for bill-paying day.

  c. Give incoming papers to the recipient for whom they are intended.

  d. Have a storage system for your children's multiple school papers.

    1. Store children's papers and projects in boxes labeled by year. Twelve boxes of the same size for twelve years pile up nicely in the corner of a bedroom.

2. Check through kids' papers for notes from teachers, report cards, and other pertinent information.

3. Encourage child to go through his papers at the end of a school year and discard any that are not important to him.

$ How to Save Dollars for Family Fun

Ask yourselves:

● What kind of a "nest" do we truly need?

    a. Would a smaller house save your family money that could be invested in family fun, schooling, and adventure?

    b. Does every child in the house need his or her own room?

    c. Do you need both a living room and a family room?

    d. Do you need a formal dining room? How often would it be used?

    e. Could you save money if you lived closer to work? School? Church?

    f. Would a mobile home be adequate to meet your needs at least for a while? Some of them are huge and beautiful. But remember to take into consideration the insurance (which could be higher than for a conventional home), space rental, and installation fees if you are buying a new mobile home. Mobile home owners pay property taxes just like other home owners. Find out what those taxes are. In many places, mobile homes decrease in value rather than increase as do conventional homes.

g. What kind of an investment are you making? Real estate in most places increases in value year after year. And because of federal tax laws, you are able to deduct the interest you pay on your home loan. Buying a home is usually a good investment.

- What level of decorating do we really need?

  a. Decide on your family's lifestyle and decorate to that lifestyle and nothing more.

  b. When your children are grown, they probably won't remember the color of your carpet or whether it was old or new. They will remember the fun you had together as a family.

- Could we decorate for less?

  a. Television programming is currently full of decorating shows that tell you how to have an interesting (sometimes beautiful) home without spending a lot of money. What those people can do with a few tools, some paint, and some fabric is truly amazing.

  b. There are dozens of books and magazines that tell you how to do everything from faux finishes to furniture building, all at discount prices. Any home-building supply store has a section of books and magazines with instructions for making everything you need.

c. Labor is one of the big costs of decorating a home. Get together with friends for a decorating party and help each other redo your homes. It's fun and a great way to save money.

d. Teach your kids, especially teenagers, how to paint and hang wallpaper. Those are skills they can use in the future to make extra money or perhaps even create their own businesses.

● Can we save money on furniture, appliances, and flooring?

You most certainly can. There are so many ideas that I have put them in an appendix at the back of this book. See page 268.

dinnertime—
it's back

There's a big movement afoot to bring back the family dinner hour. Everyone from Oprah Winfrey to your pastor is talking about it, and believe me, sitting down at a dinner table with your children is one of the most important things you can do for your family. I know, I know, it's a big bother to set the table, cook a meal, and get everyone to show up on time. But no one ever said parenting would be easy—or convenient. Being together as a family is important, however, and there is no better way to relate as a family than to meet at the dinner table. Grandparents also can help to foster family togetherness by bringing back the once-a-week-at-grandma's-house dinner, if you live in the same vicinity. And dinner doesn't have to be linens and crystal at the dining-room table. It can be pizza in the living room in front of a fire, or a backyard picnic. Being together is what is important.

Sitting down at a dinner table with your children is one of the most important things you can do for your family.

According to the National Center on Addiction and Substance Abuse at Columbia University (www.casacolumbia.org), teens who seldom eat dinner with their parents are more likely to abuse substances than those who have family dinners most nights of the week. Spending time together at the dinner table is a good way to keep your children from becoming drug abusers.

Dr. Wade F. Horn said, "It is vital that frequent family dinners become a permanent fixture for children, not only when they are young, but throughout their teenage years."* A survey conducted by CASA in 2001 showed that there are twelve things parents can do to lower the risk of their

*National Center for Addiction and Substance Abuse at Columbia University, "The Importance of Family Dinners," November 8, 2004, http://alcoholism.about.com/cs/tipsfor parents/a/blcasa030904.htm.

children becoming substance users. High on that list was the practice of eating dinner together as a family six or seven times a week with no television and no telephone calls allowed. Instead of being distracted by a television set or talking on the phone, find out what your family has been doing all day. Use the time to discuss upcoming family events and issues. Let your children talk while you listen—really listen. Teach your kids some good manners. (Where else will they learn them?)

In another study published in *Archives of Family Medicine*, researchers found that eating dinner as a family leads to healthier eating habits. The researchers studied the eating habits of 16,000 children ages nine to fourteen years and found that those who ate dinner with their families were more likely to eat those all-important five or more servings of fruits and vegetables. Dinner is the meal where a larger intake of energy and key nutrients happens than at any other meal. At the table you can set an example of good eating for your children.

There is no better time than the dinner hour for talking and listening. "When families get together at dinnertime, they share more than just a meal—they share what's been going on in their daily lives," said Gary

Hansen, extension family sociologist in the UK College of Agriculture.

But my family hates to eat together, you may be thinking. That's because they have been trained to eat on the run. To change any habit, you'll have to work at it. And first of all, you need to be convinced that eating together is important. It will start first in *your* head. You, the parent, will have to plan dinnertime. You'll have to think about it intentionally. The rest of this chapter is dedicated to ideas for making mealtimes memorable for your family.

- First, set a regular time for dinner each night. Make sure your family knows the time in advance so they are able to schedule meetings and other activities at a time other than dinnertime.

- Let older children, with adult supervision, help with the cooking. Kids will be much more interested in food they have helped to prepare. This also becomes a big time-saver later on when kids can cook all or portions of the meal.

- If you can't eat together seven nights a week, start with three nights for family mealtimes. That's a lot better than none. And although there are lots of good reasons to meet at dinnertime, if you can't, then choose another meal. The same rules about television and the telephone apply at whatever meal you choose.

- If you are a single parent, it's more important than ever that you meet with your kids at a meal. You need focused time with your kids as much or more than a two-parent family and for all the same reasons.

● Make it a goal to have your family try at least one new food item a month. Taste is acquired. It will take repeated exposure to acquire a taste for a new food.

How to Make
Family Dinnertime
the Best Hour of the Day

So let's talk about how to make dinnertime the best time of the day. First of all, come to the table as if you are meeting with the most important people on earth — you are. If you have not been in the habit of eating together, insist everyone be at the table on time and no one gets off for any reason. It's a sacred obligation. There is no more important appointment in your week or day than gathering as a family. So everything about the dinner hour should be thought out and made special. Special food and special conversations go a long way toward building memories. A wonderful website to look at is www .puttingfamilyfirst.org.

■ *Special Food*

To make sure food at your house is great, keep a menu file. Half the work of meal preparation is figuring out what you are going to eat and if you have the ingredients to make it.

The way to know ahead of time is to keep a menu file. There are a number of ways to do this.

☀Idea 1:

One writer of menu-planning ideas says that you only need about six menu cards. On each card you record a single meal idea (such as five-hour pot roast). Then you either put the recipe for the dish on the back of the card, or you record in which cookbook and on which page the recipe for it can be found. Then you list the accompanying menu items on the front of the card: green salad, ice cream and cookies for dessert, and beverages.

Rotate these menus from week to week. If you pick favorites, family members will probably always be happy with what you serve. Save the gourmet cooking for days when you have a lot of time and just feel like doing it. If you choose this system, it is simple to pull out your menu cards to compare against your master shopping list. With a quick check you see what you already have and what you need to purchase on your next shopping trip.

☀Idea 2:

One woman puts every menu item on its own card, then mixes and matches them to make varied menus. Keep refining your cards. Keep only family-tested and -approved menus.

☀Idea 3:

I have used several systems, but the one I like best is a card system set up by main entrée for the evening meal. Divide and label your menu box with these headings: beef, chicken, ham, eggs, cheese, casseroles. On each card, write not only the type of meat but also how it is to be prepared (baked chicken, fried ham, and so forth). Also list the vegetables, salad, and other accompaniments to the meal, all the way down to beverages and condiments. I also include either the recipe or the location of the recipe on the card so no time is wasted looking for it.

☀Idea 4:

Double up your cook-ing. Find some system for cooking in bulk to save time and money. This idea is not origi-nal with me, but it is such a great idea it bears repeating here. The plan is based on the made-up word "D-O-L-O-D-O-L". Here's how it works:

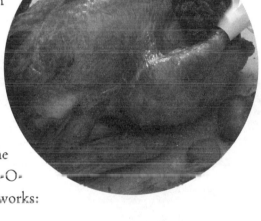

- D—Double-up cooking day (could be Saturday), when the food prepared is enough for two meals for your family. It could be a turkey or a big pot roast.

- O—One. A single-meal day.

- L—Leftover day, when a "D" meal is "re-tooled" for this meal. If you cooked a turkey before, now have turkey sandwiches or a turkey soup or casserole.

- O—One—one meal of your choice.

- D—Another double day. For example, make lasagna and freeze half of it for an "O" single day.

- O—Another one day—your choice.

- L—Use up the leftovers for the week. If there are none, go out for a hamburger.

■ More Fun Food Ideas

- Encourage your children to brainstorm ideas for dinner themes. One night might be Italian night, and all the food served follows an Italian theme. It might be St. Patrick's night, and everything is Irish and green. Let the kids help plan the menus and decorations.

- Put together a recipe book of family favorites and teach your kids how to cook those favorites.

- Take your kids shopping for food. And while you're at it, teach them how to economize and how to choose a good variety of foods, avoiding empty calories.

- Plan attractive meals by serving a variety of vegetables and fresh fruit.

88

- Find fun recipes on the Internet. You can do your own search on Google by simply typing in the words "fun recipe ideas for families." Or visit these sites: www.all recipes.com, www.5aday.com (click on the "kids" tab), www.families-first.com (click on the "recipes" tab), and www.unclebens.com (try out the "Create Your Plate" option).

- Invite extended family members to visit and cook or bring a favorite dish, perhaps one with a story behind it.

- Use the children's grandparents' or great-grandparents' recipe file.

- Teach each child to make a specialty dish that is all his own. Perhaps it is pancakes with peanuts and bananas in or on them. For another child, it may be a salad with pomegranate seeds sprinkled over the top. It doesn't matter what the dish is, just as long as each child has a contribution to make to family dinner. Teach the children to respect the offerings of other children in the family as well.

> **If you want to know what your kids are thinking about lots of topics, you will have to talk to them—and listen too.**

● Think of topics to be discussed at dinner. If you want to know what your kids are thinking about lots of topics, you will have to talk to them—and listen too.

■ Special Events

● Decide if there is something you can celebrate at dinner. Does someone have a new tooth? Did someone make it through the first day of school? Has someone hit a home run on the baseball field? Has someone survived a really horrible day at work? Is it the beginning of winter or Midsummer Day? Find something to celebrate if you can.

● If there is no event you want to celebrate at dinner, then feature conversation by having a list of conversation starters ready. You can find whole books dedicated to these. To use the web, type in "family dinner talk" in Google and see what happens. Here are some sites to look at: http://www.stouffers.com/tabletalk/index. asp?section=8&article=31, http://www.christianity today.com/cpt/2003/004/27.10.html, and http:// www.keeptalkingpublications.com/Index.htm. Or here's a list to get you started.

a. Tell about a time when you should not have laughed, but did anyway.

b. What is best about being a child? What is worst?

c. What is the earliest thing you can remember?

d. What was your most embarrassing moment?

e. If you could have dinner with anyone on earth, who would it be and why?

Here are some other fun ideas.

- Have a do-everything-backward night. Sit backward in your chair, reverse your table settings, wear your shirt backward, eat with the opposite hand from the one you usually use.

- Have an eat-with-your-hands night. This could be tied to an ethnic dinner if you choose an ethnic group who eat most of their food by picking it up with their hands.

- Have an indoor picnic and sit on a blanket on the floor.

- Grab dinner and take off for a park or beach.

- Do a truly formal dinner in your home and bring out all the china, silver, and napkins. Teach your kids how to be comfortable eating in a more formal setting.

91

A Couple of Great Food-Related Ideas

Here are two ideas about food that deserve a section of their own in this book.

■ Co-op Cooking

Co-op cooking happens when a group of people with similar needs and schedules get together to form a cooking co-op. Usually this group of people lives in the same neighborhood or at least in close proximity to each other. However, co-ops that include co-workers, church acquaintances, and other homogenous groups can work well even if the participants do not live in close proximity to each other.

A co-op begins when an interested party makes a few phone calls asking others to join the co-op. In a co-op of this kind, members take turns cooking for all the others in the group on a rotating basis. Depending on the size of the co-op, a member may only have to cook once a week. Co-op members do not eat together. Instead, meals are transported to the houses of the participants in time for their evening meals.

A co-op can share meals only four nights a week—Monday through Thursday—leaving Friday, Saturday, and Sunday for eating out, eating up leftovers, or cooking on your own. Since you cook only once a week for the co-op, anyone can see what a time-saver co-op would be. But surprise! It is also a huge money saver, because you are able to buy and use food in bulk. Bulk food is always less expensive.

92

If you are a member of a co-op but it is not your night to cook, your meal will be delivered to your door. All you need to do is heat up the food (if not delivered hot); unwrap the salad, vegetables, and dessert; set the table; and sit down with your family to a home-cooked meal you didn't have to prepare. Of course, you will have to take your turn cooking for all the other families, and that can take half a day.

To make a co-op work smoothly, some up-front questions need to be asked. They are basically:

- Are our tastes in food compatible?
- How much food is enough for each family?
- Who will deliver the food and when?
- Do we need to meet occasionally to discuss how our co-op is working? Where and how often?

Here are some additional benefits to co-op cooking.

- By planning menus ahead, you can take advantage of sales and buying in bulk.
- You save a lot of time in the grocery store because you are only buying for one meal's preparation—fewer ingredients to search for, less time in the store, big time savings.
- You will save money because you won't be impulse buying easy-to-prepare or ready-made foods.

- Because the co-op members meet and plan menus together, you are done figuring out what to cook until the next meeting.

- Your kitchen only gets messy once a week. Allow three or four hours' cooking time on this day.

- Instead of dinnertime stress, you will have lots of time to enjoy a meal with laughter and smiles.

- You can pour a lot of creative energy into that one meal you cook each week. Get out the cookbooks and be creative.

- Co-op cooking creates a sense of community—something sadly lacking in our busy world today.

> Co-op cooking creates a sense of community—something sadly lacking in our busy world today.

- Anyone can do this, even if you do not consider yourself a cook. Start with simple menus (spaghetti and salad, for instance). Ask for help and advice from your friends who love to cook. Before you know it, co-op cooking will become a way of life.

Here are some websites to help you get started: http://dinnercoop.cs.cmu.edu/dinnercoop/, http://www.recipegal.com/links/co-opcooking.html, and http://www.stretcher

.com/stories/00/000508d.cfm. A good book to get is *Home-made To Go, The Complete Guide to Co-op Cooking,* by Dee Sarton Bower, available through Amazon.com.

◼ *Gleaning*

On a recent trip to Se-attle, I found my three nieces (young women with growing families and tight budgets) involved in gleaning. I thought I knew what gleaning was. After all, in the Bible land-owners were instructed to not harvest the corners of their fields so that the poor could come in and glean for their needs. But I had much to learn about today's gleaning practices.

A side effect of our affluent society is that every community would waste tons and tons of food if it were not for gleaners. Gleaners gather up this excess food and distribute it to those in need. As a bonus for their labor, they are entitled to shop at the distribution center free of charge. My nieces estimate they are saving about four hundred dollars a month on food for their families. And they are investing about twenty-four hours a month to make that savings.

Gleaners have a regular route they follow to pick up food items that are near their due dates. Milk, juices, meat, and produce are all perishable and must be moved quickly. In addition, any nonperishable items that a store wants to clear out may also be put aside for the gleaners. Store personnel put items for gleaners in a shopping cart and leave it in a designated place. Gleaners wear a badge for identification. They move the shopping carts out of the store in the manner each store requests and load everything into their cars. Certain designated gleaners also pick up bread from bakeries and extra food from restaurants every day. Everything is taken to a distribution center—which may be in someone's garage— where it is sorted by other volunteers. In the gleaning organization in Seattle, the abundance of the gleaning (and there is a huge amount) is given to charitable organizations.

Each gleaning operation operates a little differently. In Ventura County, California, gleaners (often senior citizens) go to the fields and harvest leftover produce. About fifty to sixty thousand pounds of produce is harvested each month. In addition, gleaners also gather items from grocery stores, coffee shops, and other places where food is sold or prepared.

In a gleaning operation, everyone wins. The poor and hungry are fed, and there is plenty left for the gleaners. Store owners get tax breaks for their contributions and don't have to pay for disposal of produce and other goods. All store personnel must do is put grocery items in a cart and put the cart in a designated spot. And in the case of one of my nieces, her animals benefit as well. After bread is no longer fit for human consumption, she takes what's left to feed her barnyard animals. The animals love the stale bread, and Karen saves on expensive feed.

If you can't go to the fields to pick produce, most gleaning operations have plenty of jobs that must be done to keep things running smoothly. So if you have more time than money, investigate gleaning.

⌛ How to Save Time for Family Fun

- Find a system of menu planning that works for you and stick to it. It is stress-reducing to know what's for dinner. You can concentrate your efforts on making the dinner hour special for family members.

- Keep a menu file, but do not keep every recipe ever invented. Your family will have favorites, and you can prepare them again and again and never hear a complaint. Using familiar recipes is easier than trying new ones. You will already know the ingredients and the procedures.

- Create and shop with a master grocery list. Nothing wastes more time with regard to food than frequent shopping. A co-worker of mine once said, "I stop at the grocery store every night on my way home. I never know what I want to eat until then." She had no children, and so it was possible for her to stop every night on her way home, but for most of us that would completely upset everyone for the evening. Better to shop as seldom as possible and shop with a master list keyed to your menu planning.

● Create your master list by taking a pad and pencil to the store and, following your usual route through the store, writing down the names of items you frequently use. You don't need to look at twenty-seven kinds of dishwashing soap if you have a favorite. List its location and save time by going straight to it and picking it up. (By the way, it helps to shop the same store every time.) Don't forget a reminder to yourself to check the ends of the aisles for bargains and to look in hidden corners where marked-down items are kept. When you are satisfied with your list, type it out and post a copy in an obvious place in your kitchen. (Store your master list on your computer and run multiple copies.) When you run out of something, circle the item on your

> **Shop as seldom as possible and shop with a master list keyed to your menu planning.**

chart or otherwise mark it for your next shopping trip. Then remember to take your list with you to the store and save all kinds of time and also money. A master list keeps you from wandering aimlessly around looking for things, and it will keep you away from tempting foods that call to you, "Buy me. Buy me."

● To save time, learn how all your cooking equipment works and use it. Use your microwave, your oven, your rice cooker to full advantage. You don't need to babysit your appliances.

$ How to Save Dollars for Family Fun

Here are some food-saving tips. You'll find lots more in the "Quick Guide to Saving Money" on page 255.

● Leave the family at home. They can sabotage a food budget.

● Sugared cereals are more expensive by far. Buy the plain variety and sweeten it at home.

● Mix your own salad dressings from packaged mixes. You'll save significantly over bottled dressings.

● Watch the meat counters for marked-down meat. Buy it in bulk to freeze at home.

- Use soy veggie crumbles instead of meat. It's good for you and less expensive than ground hamburger.

- When buying a turkey, pick a large one. You get more meat per pound on a bird weighing twelve or more pounds.

- Consider joining a co-op or food gleaning group.

- Learn to use herbs and spices to flavor inexpensive dishes.

- Eat at home. Restaurant food is expensive.

- Join a warehouse club to buy food in bulk. But buy carefully. It is not a bargain if you can't use up what you buy.

- Consider planting a garden and learning to preserve food for later use.

5

treasured guests

Whatever you do, don't miss the wonderful opportunities that come when you invite guests into your home. I remember one of my son's birthdays. It happened on a Sunday, and we had invited guests for dinner. There at our table were a missionary couple to Greece, a college student who was serving an internship, our son's grandmother, and a couple who had brought a wonderful birthday cake decorated with clowns. It was just right for a little boy's third birthday.

The conversation at that table and the interest shown to my three-year-old began something wonderful in his heart. Before he was twenty, he had been on several ministry trips, some of them overseas. From small beginnings at our dining-room table and the trips he took, he gained a broader, more caring worldview and a concern for others.

The Importance of Having Guests in Your Home

I think entertaining others in your home is one of the finest activities a family can pursue. Here's why.

◼ *Entertaining Guests Is Biblical*

The idea of hospitality is found throughout the Bible. In the Middle Eastern culture of the Bible, the attitude toward hospitality was that once a guest entered your home, everything you had was his. It was as if he owned it (which is a bit further than most of us want to go). "Do not forget to entertain strangers, for by so doing some people have entertained angels without knowing it" (Heb. 13:2 NIV). This is probably a reference to Genesis 18, when Abraham was visited by three men who were either angels or angels and a preincarnate Christ. When Abraham, sitting by his tent in the heat of the day, saw the three approaching, he ran to them and offered them a place to rest, water to bathe their feet, and a meal. At the end of the visit, they confided to Abraham that he was about to become a father. And it was so.

Guests Can Teach

Your guests become teachers of your children and can provide a wonderful learning experience for them, especially if you thoughtfully invite guests with special knowledge and talents. There are artists and musicians and storytellers who could bring delight and wonder to our children's lives. Invite a nurse, a guitar teacher, an actress, a drummer, or a painter. And there are older people who feel life has gone on without them and they no longer have value to anyone. Their stories of life in earlier times will stretch your children's imaginations and broaden their understanding of the past. If you have invited guests with talents, ask them to perform their special talents. You might tell the guests ahead of time that you will ask them and why you are asking. Before these guests come to dinner or dessert, have your children write out questions regarding your visitors' abilities or memories.

■ Guests Give Cross-Cultural Exposure

Your children can experience a world culture without ever leaving home. Your table can become the crossroads of the world. Colleges and universities are full of homesick international students who would love to be invited to an American home. There are also American kids who are away from home for the first time and would enjoy a home-cooked meal. Even if these students are only from the next state, your children can learn something new from them.

> Your table can become the crossroads of the world.

■ Guests Can Share Career Ideas with Your Children

There are people who travel for a living who would be delighted to spend a night in a home instead of yet another hotel. There are business associates who would respond in a relaxed, positive way if they could share a meal at your table. They too bring information and stories to enrich your children's lives. These guests might be particularly appropriate if you have young teens who are researching possibilities for lifetime careers. This would be a good time for them to get firsthand information about a career idea.

104

■ *Guests Can Include Key People*

Having guests is the best way for your children to get to know key people in their lives with whom they might not have personal contact. For example, invite your pastor and his family into your home. This is a wonderful way for your children to know your pastor and his family as people rather than just public figures. You'll soon learn they laugh like you do, they cry too, they get hurt, and they enjoy success. Teach your children to admire and respect your pastor. This will be easier if they know him.

■ *Having Guests Teaches Your Children about Hospitality*

Being hospitable teaches your children about hospitality in the best way—by example. There is a warm sense of sharing what you have with others that breeds generosity in your children. Caring, genuine interest in others, and appreciation for abilities and talent are just some of the things that come when families share their table with others.

Where Do I Begin?

1. *First decide if you really want to have guests.* Even after you've considered all I've said about guests being a positive experience for your children, if you are miserable having guests, neither you, your children, nor your guests will have a good time. So know your limits.

105

2. *If you do want to entertain, planning is the next stage.* Some people have just one event of the same kind once a year, and that is the extent of their entertaining. They've decided that's the limit of what they can do.

3. *Begin your planning with the food.* Remember that people have a good time when they have good food to eat. Become famous for just one or two dishes. Keep a few items in your cupboard from which you can whip up a specialty meal. It could be something as simple as a spectacular omelet or an awesome salad. Make and keep a shopping list of everything you will need for entertaining guests.

4. *If people ask to bring food—let them.* You should prepare the main dish and make it ahead of time if possible. Stick with simple foods that are easily prepared. Again, you want to be able to enjoy your guests by spending time with them and not staying in the kitchen cooking.

5. *Ask yourself if you need more serving dishes.* If so, see if you can borrow from a friend or neighbor, or check out a discount store or even a thrift shop for inexpensive dishes to buy.

6. *Don't invite more people than your house can comfortably handle.* It's not fun to have someone's elbow in your ribs when you are trying to get a fork full of food to your mouth. Better to have two parties than crowd too many people into one.

7. *Set the tone.* What kind of party atmosphere do you want? Silly and fun? Lovely and candlelit? Down home?

Barbecue? You decide, and I can assure you your guests will enjoy whatever you decide.

How to Be a Great Host

I can just hear you now. "I have an eight-to-five job and an hour commute, and you want me to think about having company? Saturday is the day I do everything that doesn't get done during the week, and Sunday is my only day to recover before I start again. I don't know when I'd find time to entertain."

Somewhere along the way, possibly because there are so many television programs about how to have the perfect home and how to be the perfect host and hostess, we've forgotten the real intent of hospitality. It is to be with people we care about. Don't be cowed by television personalities whose real intent is to sell you products. Don't believe that you have to have the latest thing in appliances, a new china pattern in a certain color, and tablecloths, napkins, and candles galore. Hospitality is not about things or an abundance

Hospitality is not about things or an abundance of things. It is simply about breaking bread with someone you care about.

107

of things. It is simply about breaking bread with someone you care about. It doesn't have to be complicated and wearing on you and your family. Simple is good and can even be delightful.

Tips for Being a Great Host

- *Keep your entertaining simple.* Some of my favorite hours these days are when I call a neighbor at the last minute and say, "Come on over for soup, bread, and a salad. We'll eat in the courtyard by candlelight." What could be better?

- *Focus on your guests while respecting your children.* I recently visited in the home of a family where we ate in the dining room. The host had prepared a delicious meal, and there were candles on the table. That was all wonderful, but what I remember most was his interaction with his children at that table. He gave them, even the youngest one, time to tell stories, ask questions, and express opinions. In other words, he respected his children. That's the treasure I took away from that evening. It gave me a sense of solidity about his family and their values.

- *Don't do all the work.* If you've been letting your kids learn how to help in the kitchen, they can be of great assistance when it comes to preparing food and serving guests. What better way to learn how to be hospitable than by assisting you? Kids can set the table, make the salad, and carry dishes back and forth to the kitchen.

- *Give your house a quick once-over for cleaning.* Pick up anything lying around and get it out of sight. Stuffing it in a box in the closet is fine for now. Dust a little and run the vacuum if needed. That's enough. Don't give a second thought to your furnishings. They are just fine. If people are coming just to see your house and your furnishings, you've invited the wrong people.

- *Encourage drop-in guests.* Every family has to decide what they are comfortable with on this one, but often children have friends over to play, and when dinnertime comes, it's nice to invite them to stay for dinner if their parents approve. If I have visitors show up at a mealtime, they are welcome to eat at my table, but they'll have to eat what is prepared.

Plan a Dinner Party

For a dinner party, get as much ready beforehand as possible. The more you have ready, the more time you will have to enjoy yourself with your guests.

■ *One to Two Weeks Ahead*

1. Shop early for nonperishable food items and supplies. Store them all together in a designated place and declare them off-limits to the family.

2. If it fits in with your menu plan, make and freeze casseroles and desserts to thaw on the day of the event.

■ *The Day before Your Dinner Party*

3. Shop for fresh ingredients and last-minute items.

4. Cut or slice any ingredients you will be using and put them in lock-top bags the night before they are needed.

5. Marinate anything that needs to be marinated.

6. Slice the bread and wrap tightly in foil, ready to be heated in the oven and served.

7. Put condiments in their serving dishes and cover them tightly with plastic wrap. Put them in the refrigerator until just before you serve the meal.

8. Make sure you have enough ice on hand.

9. On a sideboard or even on the table, set out all your dishware and linens. If dust or pets are a problem, drop a clean sheet over everything to protect it until time to set the table.

10. The actual set-up can be done the day before your party. It's good to get this out of the way ahead of time. Move the furniture and set the table, except for a floral arrangement if you are using live flowers. Completely cover everything with a clean sheet to keep it spotless. If you have a buffet or side table, set up the dessert table with plates, forks, napkins, coffee cups, cream, and sugar. Cover it also. Let me discourage the use of

a kids' table. It defeats the purpose of having guests in your home so that your children can learn from them.

▋ *The Day of the Party*

11. Have the coffeepot ready to go at the push of a button.

12. As much as you can, assemble and prepare food early in the day.

13. Set out all the serving dishes and serving utensils.

14. Run the dishwasher to clean up as many dishes as possible beforehand. Just make sure the dishwasher is empty when guests arrive.

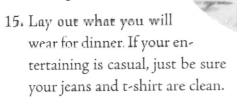

15. Lay out what you will wear for dinner. If your entertaining is casual, just be sure your jeans and t-shirt are clean.

16. Load your stereo with the music you plan to play and set the volume.

17. If you are expecting children accompanying adults, remove breakables from any room where they will be. Move your valuable items to a safe place.

111

18. Do a quick check of your bathrooms. Make sure they are adequately stocked with soap, towels, toilet paper, and a votive candle or two.

When You Have Overnight Houseguests

Having overnight houseguests can put quite a strain on a family if you are not used to it. (It strains the houseguests too.) But a little preparation can make this time wonderful for everyone involved. Here are some tips for making your overnight hospitality work smoothly.

- *Make up your mind to relax and enjoy your guests.* Don't strive for perfection. You'll never achieve it, and you'll only make yourself and everyone around you miserable. Make having houseguests more about them than about you. What would they like to do? Where would they like to go?

- *Adapt an attitude that says, "Mi casa es su casa."* My house is your house. Your guests are not going to do serious damage to your house, so don't worry about it. So what if you need to retouch the paint in the hallways or have the carpets cleaned after your guests go? I knew a woman who waited to clean until after her guests had departed. Maybe that's a good idea.

- *Treat your guests like a new puppy, as someone has suggested.* Give them their own space, not too much excitement, and not too much talk. Spend time with your guests and give them affection and caring, but don't overdo it. Expect them to need time for themselves away from the routines of your household.

- *Ask about any allergies that might affect the quality of your guests' visit.* And while you're at it, ask about any food preferences they or their children have. Do they hate fish? Must a child have toast with peanut butter for breakfast?

- *Prepare the guest room as if for yourself.* What do you need in your room to be comfortable? Here are some essentials.

  a. Clean linens.

  b. A water glass and a pitcher of water.

  c. Extra pillows of varying thicknesses.

  d. An extra blanket or two.

  e. Some current magazines.

  f. A scented candle if the guest is not allergic to scents.

  g. A comfortable chair.

  h. Clothes hangers and a place to hang clothing.

  i. A drawer for clothing if the stay is more than a couple of days.

113

j. A stand for suitcases (or a designated place for open luggage) if the guest will not be unpacking.

k. Room-darkening shades if possible.

■ Plan Simple and More Elaborate Meals for Guests

● *Have a pot of homemade soup simmering on the stove when overnight guests arrive.* Good soup, great bread, and a comfortable bed get the visit off to a nice start. Save your gourmet meal for a time when all of you are rested. If you make a big pot of soup, you will have it ready for lunches later during your guests' stay.

● *Fix simple meals for kids.* Kids appreciate simple meals. Have frozen pizza dough and a variety of toppings on hand and let them make their own pizza. This works for fajitas, tacos, and other "self-assembled" dishes too.

● *Have at least one really big casserole frozen and ready to pop in the oven.*

● *Keep healthy snacks available for kids.* Bowls of popcorn without butter and carrot and celery sticks are a good start.

● *Ice cream with a choice of toppings is a dessert for kids that can't be beat.* If the kids are lactose intolerant or if the parents want the kids eating only superhealthy foods, try soy ice cream. It's healthy and delicious.

114

■ *If Your Guests Have Little Ones*

Here's how to make your home safe for a child.

- Put up baby gates at the top and bottom of stairs and use them all the time there are small children in the home.

- Check under sinks and in bathroom cabinets and lock up all dangerous and poisonous items.

- Install baby locks on cabinet doors where hazardous products are kept.

- Check your outdoor play equipment for loose parts and make sure it is safe.

- Put corner protectors on the sharp edges of furniture.

- Turn your water temperature down to a safe level. The maximum should be 120 degrees.

- Put protective covers into outlets to keep prying fingers out of them.

- Install door or window safety locks/hardware especially on upper floors (older children must be able to operate the locks). Get some cleats to secure curtain cords and train yourself to use them.

- If your stairway and balcony railings are at a width little ones could slip through or get their heads stuck between, tie canvas or acrylic panels over them.

- Post emergency numbers on or next to the phone. Since your guests don't know your town, put a family

115

doctor's number and an emergency hospital number by the phone as well. A map to the nearest emergency facility would be a good idea. Print one out from the Internet.

When Your Guests Arrive

The tone you set when first greeting guests to your home, whether they are overnight guests or dinner guests, is important. Go to the door to greet them, even if it means coming in from the patio where you have been grilling their dinner or turning off the stove in the kitchen. Make them feel welcome.

When your guests first arrive, find out their preferences for breakfast.

- What time do they like to have breakfast?

- What do they like to eat for breakfast?

- Perhaps show them where cereals and pastries are kept and invite them to help themselves if they are early risers. Or just set up a buffet of cereals, yogurt, baked goods, milk, coffee, tea, and juice.

116

- If they will be getting up before you do, show them how the coffeepot works. Have it ready for them to just push a button.

Remember that your way of doing things is just that—your way of doing things. If you want your guests to feel at home, don't try to impose your rules and regulations on them unless it is a health issue, such as smoking in the house, or a moral issue. You have a right to make such rules for the sake of your family.

If you want your guests to feel at home, don't try to impose your rules and regulations on them unless it is a health issue or a moral issue.

Show overnight guests where they will stay and point out the bathroom they are to use. If they have been traveling any distance, they will be very grateful not to have to ask for the bathroom. Take the coats of dinner guests and put them away.

State the rules. "Help yourself to anything in the refrigerator anytime you like." If there are rules that just have to be kept, such as "Don't let the dog out for any reason," let your guests know right up front.

117

■ What Extra Activities Shall We Plan?

It's the eternal question, isn't it, especially if you have kids as house guests? You will need to plan some activities for your guests. Water is a surefire attraction for kids. Whether it's a real swimming pool, a small wading pool, an ocean or lake beach, or water in buckets, water and kids just go together. So if it's summer and you can do it, get the kids to water.

What attractions are in your area? Would your guests like to visit them? Is cost a factor? How many attractions are enough? One of the most fun things I ever experienced was in New Orleans when my hostess handed me a tape and a tape player and told me to walk through her neighborhood playing the tape. On it was a homemade tour describing the old houses and their history, the trees, and the above-ground cemeteries found in New Orleans. Could you turn your guests loose to walk around your town and learn the history of the place you call home? Several short excursions might work better than daylong tours, especially if there are young children in the group.

Just because you have grown used to local attractions doesn't mean they wouldn't be interesting to someone else. Almost every town has some kind of attraction. My hometown of Deer Lodge, Montana, has two very prominent sites of interest. One is the Grant-Kohrs ranch—a working ranch that dates from another century. It is a national historic site. The other is the old territorial prison. It is right on the main street of the town and is no longer used to house prisoners.

118

Now tours are conducted throughout the summer. Check to see what your town has to offer.

⧗ How to Save Time for Family Fun

● *Don't cook.* Cooking takes a lot of time. Find meals your family and guests will love that can be put together in a hurry and don't require cooking. Here are three suggestions.

a. Main-dish salad pita sandwiches: Combine salad greens (lettuce, arugula, spinach) and any kind of precooked meat. Meat can be left over from another meal or purchased ready-cooked. Add roasted red peppers and mayonnaise and spoon the mixture into a whole-wheat pita. Or forget the pita and just eat the salad and serve bread or chips on the side.

b. Chicken fajitas: Top whole-wheat tortillas with slices of precooked chicken breast, green bell peppers, and red onion; serve with fat-free sour cream and salsa. You can warm the meat and the tortillas in the microwave for about forty seconds if you prefer a warm fajita.

c. Wraps: Spread a whole-wheat tortilla with spicy mustard (if your kids like it); top with smoked turkey breast or roasted chicken or tuna, cheese slices, shredded lettuce, and sliced tomato. Roll it up. You might want to cut it in half for your kids.

● *Cook a little bit.* Everyone loves pizza, but it is time-consuming to make unless you do it this way. Buy a ready-made pizza shell or Boboli bread. If you have a lot of guests, you'd better buy two large ones. Also buy a can of pizza sauce and a large package of shredded mozzarella cheese. Then go to the salad bar of your local supermarket and pick just those items you really love on pizza. You may find pepperoni slices, ham pieces, or other meats. You will find sliced mushrooms, olives, artichoke hearts, onions, tomatoes, pineapple, and other yummies for pizza. It doesn't matter if you dump all these ingredients together in the box provided by the store. When you get home, unwrap the bread and put it on the baking sheet. Spread it with pizza sauce, dump the contents of the salad box on top, and arrange the pieces if you wish. Top with the shredded cheese and pop it in a hot oven for about twenty minutes. Dinner's ready.

● *Cook one-dish dinners for big time savings.* Here's a great site for one-dish dinners: www.kraftfoods.com (type "one-dish" in the search box). This site also has ideas for kids' meals, energy meals, healthy eating, and great desserts. It also has innovative recipe search op-

120

tions, such as "enter ingredients," "search by meal occasion," and "recipe type."

- *Beg, buy, or barter for time.* If company is coming and you are swamped for time, trade something with a neighbor to help you out. If you develop an attitude of helping others and being helped by others, life will become much simpler.

> **If you develop an attitude of helping others and being helped by others, life will become much simpler.**

  a. Swap babysitting so you can get ready for your event without kids underfoot.

  b. Borrow dishes or table linens.

  c. Get your neighbor to do a centerpiece for you in exchange for some talent you have.

- You can actually save time by keeping your home in tip-top shape.

  a. Here is a wonderful website with loads of tips on how to be always ready for guests: http://www.demesne .info/Home-Maintenance/March-Maintenance.htm. It has a monthly checklist of things to do for home maintenance.

  b. For tips galore, go to "Ask Jeeves" (www.askjeeves .com) and type in the word "homemaker." You will get twenty pages of websites related to keeping a home.

$ How to Save Dollars for Family Fun

- One kind of entertaining with costs that can quickly get out of hand is kids' birthday parties. For loads of inexpensive, easy entertaining ideas for kids' parties, go to:

  a. http://www.essortment.com/in/Children.Parties.Activities/

  b. http://www.childrensparties.com.au/pages/default.cfm?page_id=5648

  c. http://www.kidspartysurvivalguide.com/

- Another kind of entertaining that easily becomes expensive is dinners with lots of guests. Usually you know a long time before one of these events when it will happen. To save money, watch sales at local supermarkets and when a main-dish item, such as a pot roast, comes on sale, buy and freeze. Buy large turkeys rather than small ones to get the most for your money. You can freeze what's left over for smaller family dinners.

family seasoning—
celebrate every
holiday

There, in the presence of the LORD your God, you and your families shall eat and shall rejoice in everything you have put your hand to, because the LORD your God has blessed you.

Deuteronomy 12:7 NIV

You work hard. Whether you are the breadwinner and go to a job every day or the one who keeps the home fires burning, you are fully occupied in providing for your family. You contribute finances, whether by earning them or saving them. You labor physically, whether by sitting at a desk plugging away or carrying laundry up and down the stairs. You are continually improving your investments, whether you are putting money into an account that grows or improving your house and yard. All work is good, and it should bring a great deal of satisfaction as you care for your home and family. But there needs to be a time for rewards.

Family celebrations are one of the rewards of faithful services. More than trophies that only collect dust, more than monetary rewards that are soon spent, family celebrations are rewards that will be remembered for a lifetime. So celebrate. Celebrate everything—birthdays, special occasions, anniversaries, beginnings, and endings. Enjoy life, enjoy your family, and enjoy the fruits of your labor.

Family celebrations are one more time to teach your kids your values and help them understand they are part of a larger plan. Your children are pieces of a family that has a great history and far-reaching possibilities for the future. Teach your kids that they are an important link in the chain of life and of your family. They are the hope for the future of your family.

> **Your children are pieces of a family that has a great history and far-reaching possibilities for the future.**

Make family celebrations your very own. Don't be sucked into doing it the way others in your family have done it or the way some television personality says you should celebrate. When a couple marries, the two individuals will bring traditions from their families.

124

Make those traditions the starting point for building your own family unit. Included in building your own traditions is permission not to spend every holiday at someone else's house. Your kids need to spend time with you in your own home. So stay home with your children and enjoy them. They will be gone before you know it.

Celebrations don't have to be expensive to be great, but you will want to save for bigger experiences and adventures than you can find at home (such as trips and theme parks). Let's see how family celebrations can be wonderful, inexpensive, and memorable for your kids. We'll start with the biggest holiday of all, Christmas, and work our way through the year.

Advent

Advent begins the Sunday after Thanksgiving. Advent is another way to focus on the true meaning of Christmas.

■ A Candle Advent Celebration

For this observance, you'll need an Advent wreath with five candles. You can purchase wreaths at church-supply stores or make your own. (See instructions below.)

There are many opinions about the proper color of Advent candles. Some people use four red ones around the outside and a white one in the middle. Others use pink candles around the outside and a purple one in the middle. The point is that the

125

one different candle is used to represent the Christ child and the other candles represent the four symbols of Advent.

There are also different teachings about the significance of each candle. One interpretation is that the first candle represents the prophets who foretold Christ's birth; the second represents Mary, the mother of Christ; the third represents Joseph; the fourth represents the shepherds; and the middle candle represents Christ.

How to Make Your Own Advent Wreath

Insert candles into a Styrofoam circle that has been covered with sprigs of evergreen or holly. (Remember, never leave burning candles unattended and replace those that burn down close to the wreath.) If you construct your own wreath, make it a family holiday project. Send everyone to search for greens or let them purchase them at the store.

First Week: Prophecy Candle

It is important that your children know Christ's birth was prophesied long before he came. His coming was planned by God from the beginning of all things. Here is a partial list of Scriptures that prophesied his coming:

126

Genesis 3:15

Isaiah 7:14

Isaiah 9:1–2, 6–7

Isaiah 52:13–53:12

Malachi 3:1

Read several of these Scriptures together and talk about what you have read. Then one person should light the first candle. Sing a Christmas carol or two. Blow out the candle and leave the wreath where the whole family can see it.

Second Week: Mary Candle

The second candle is for Mary, the mother of Jesus. Read together the story of Gabriel's announcement to her in Luke 1:26–38. Help your children understand that Mary was being given the highest honor any woman could ever have—to become the mother of the Savior of the world.

Light the prophecy candle again and have a second family member light the candle for Mary. Then sing appropriate Christmas carols.

The story of Gabriel's announcement would be a good one for the family to dramatize. Put on bathrobes and towels for head coverings. Let one person be the angel who announced the good news to Mary.

Talk about what happened to Mary. Why did the angel tell her not to be afraid? How do your family members think Mary felt? Why was Mary so willing to become the mother of Jesus? If your children are old enough, talk about the stigma attached to this event. Explain that Mary, although engaged, was not yet married. Explain what that would mean in her culture. Pray together and thank God for sending Jesus.

Third Week: Joseph Candle

The third candle represents Joseph. Read Matthew 1:18–25 in which Joseph is told about Jesus's birth.

Have family members relight the first two candles and then have a third family member light the Joseph candle. Sing appropriate carols. Once again, family members could act out the story.

Discuss how Joseph must have felt when he saw the angel. Be sure your children understand that God is the heavenly Father of Jesus and that God entrusted Jesus and Mary into Joseph's care. You will have to tailor this discussion to the ages of your children.

Fourth Week: Shepherd Candle

Read Luke 2:8–20, the story of the angels' pronouncement to the shepherds in the fields.

Relight the first three candles. (You may have to replace some of them by now.) Sing appropriate Christmas carols.

Talk together about why the shepherds were in the fields. Emphasize that they were the first to greet the new baby lying in a manger. Discuss their humble attitude, our attitude toward Jesus, and the importance of adoring Jesus Christ.

Spend time together praying. Encourage the children to make statements of adoration to Christ.

Christmas Day: Christ Candle

Christmas Day is the last day of Advent. Read the passage about the birth of Christ in Luke 2:1–7. Relight all four candles and, together as a family, light the center candle, which represents Jesus. Sing Christmas carols together. Have each person express gratitude to God in prayer for his gift of Jesus. Pray together and rejoice that Christ is born. Let the candles burn throughout Christmas.

■ A Nativity Advent Celebration

Some families celebrate Advent with a Bible-reading program similar to the one listed earlier, but instead of using candles, they use the figures of the nativity scene to play out the Christmas story.

First Week: Prophecy (The Empty Manger)

The first week, the empty manger is placed in a prominent position—low enough so the littlest children in the family can see it. The idea is to move the figures toward the manger scene a little each week. The first week uses no figures because prophecy is a foretelling of something no one has yet seen. Read the same Scriptures as the first week of the Candle Advent and talk about prophecy in general. Talk about the people who watched and waited for the Messiah.

Second Week: Mary

The second week, place Mary somewhere in the room but not at the manger. Place an angel near her when you read the story of the announcement. Use the same carols and readings as those given in the second week of the Candle Advent.

Third Week: Joseph

The third week, place Joseph near Mary and the angel figure nearby. Read the Scriptures relating to Joseph and the angel's announcement to him. Sing appropriate carols and pray together.

Fourth Week: Shepherds

The fourth week, add the shepherd figures somewhere in the room. Read and talk about Joseph and Mary's journey to Bethlehem. Let the children move the figures of Mary and Joseph closer and closer to the manger through the devotional time. Then finally place these figures by the manger.

Christmas Day: Baby Jesus

On Christmas Day, let the children place the Christ child in the manger. Read the appropriate Scriptures and sing carols. Bring the angel figures to the shepherds to make their announcement. After this, bring the shepherds and angels to the nativity scene.

Christmas

Is there a man, woman, boy, or girl alive who does not love Christmas? And yet, Christmas can be a time of extreme stress if parents do not slow down and enjoy their children and their home during this season. Do everything you can to keep a calm atmosphere that honors Christ throughout this holiday season.

> **Christmas can be a time of extreme stress if parents do not slow down and enjoy their children and their home during this season.**

■ *Decorate*

Have a traditional day for decorating the tree, such as the day after Thanksgiving. Invite others to help decorate your tree, especially if they cannot have a tree. Make a special event out of it.

Decorate to a Theme

● *Animals:* One year your theme could be the animals of Christmas. Let the children bring out all their stuffed animals as part of the display. Help the children cut out shapes of animals from stiff construction paper and hang them on the tree. For Christmas dinner, serve a cake that is shaped like an animal.

● *The Nutcracker:* Another year you could decorate to a nutcracker theme. Take the kids to see *The Nutcracker* performed. Buy a nutcracker figure to keep as a memento of this Christmas. Let the kids perform their own version of *The Nutcracker.* Play a soundtrack from *The Nutcracker* ballet.

● *Pick a country:* Choose a country of the world that has different Christmas traditions from those you normally celebrate. Invite guests from that culture for dinner. Scour cookbooks for recipes from that country. Learn what decorations are traditionally used in that country. Does the country celebrate on the same day as your family, or is it earlier or later?

● *Angels:* An angel theme is especially nice. Cut paper angels from stiff, white construction paper and hang them all around the house. Read the Christmas story

132

with special emphasis on how the angels were involved in our Savior's birth. Serve angel food cake.

Decorate the Whole House

- Decorate every nook and cranny of your house.

- Have a box of decorations for each child's room and let the children decorate at their leisure.

- Decorate outside as well with food for small animals and birds.

- Lots of little white lights are a delight to the eyes of both children and adults. Use them in the trees outside, in the windows, and all around the house.

■ Celebrate

Determine in your heart that your family's Christmas celebration will focus on Jesus. After all, he is the reason for the season. There are dozens of ways for making Jesus the focal point of your Christmas celebrations.

Start the first year your baby can sit up and take part in the celebration by planning a birthday party for Jesus. Decorate a cake together. Put birthday candles on it.

Remember also to make your Christmas a time of "other-centeredness." Here are some ideas.

- Think what you could do for people who cannot get out or are alone for Christmas. Make gifts for these people, wrap them, and deliver them on or before Christmas.

- Work together before Christmas to earn money to support a child in a foreign country through a qualified agency.

- Write cards and letters to family and friends. Do it as a Christmas project.

- If your children are older, volunteer at a shelter during the Christmas season. It will be an experience they won't forget.

Epiphany or Twelfth Night

Epiphany, celebrated on January 6, is the traditional holiday that celebrates the revealing of Christ to the Gentiles, represented by the wise men from the east. In some countries this, rather than Christmas, is the day for giving gifts. In many places of the world, it is considered the conclusion of the Christmas season.

I was recently in a home where parents put up the Christmas tree on Christmas Eve and it remained in place until Epiphany. Whether you choose to do this or not, Epiphany is a nice ending to the Christmas holiday celebration for your family.

If you used a nativity scene for Advent, read the story of the wise men and move their figures to where you have placed the figures of Mary, Joseph, and the baby—not in the stable. Explain to your children that the wise men probably did not come to see the Christ child until he was about two years old and living in a house.

In our family, at Epiphany, we gathered together and read all the Christmas cards we had received during the holiday. Sometimes we had been too busy to read them carefully when they arrived. We chose the cards we considered the prettiest, the funniest, the most meaningful, and so on. We usually played our Christmas music one more time and read the portion of the Christmas story that tells about the visit of the wise men to Bethlehem. We sang "We Three Kings of Orient Are." And if there were any leftover Christmas goodies, we consumed them during this family time. The next morning, we removed the Christmas tree and all other decorations and packed everything away for another year.

Easter

Perhaps the most important holiday of the year for a Christian family is Easter. Because of the resurrection, we have a hope and a future. In a war-infested, poverty-ridden, disease-suffering world, our children need to know the hope that Christ lives. Easter can be a shared experience through which we emphasize, again and again, the importance of our relationship with God. We value Jesus Christ. We value the cross and the finished work of Calvary. We need to pass those values on to our children.

> **Because of the resurrection, we have a hope and a future.**

Sometime during the holiday, sit down together and read the Easter story. If your children can read, let them participate. If they can't, choose a Bible storybook with pictures that is simple enough for them to understand. As you share this reading time together, remember that the story you are reading is the most important one in the Bible—the most important one in all history. Take time for it.

■ *Ways to Celebrate Easter*

● *Color eggs*: Most children love coloring Easter eggs. Do it as a family and be creative. You may want to hide eggs on Easter afternoon and let the kids hunt for them.

On Easter Sunday, after church and dinner, we played in the yard with the kids (weather permitting) and hid eggs everywhere—although our shaggy gray poodle often gave away the hiding places. The children never tired of having us hide the eggs, and they enjoyed hiding eggs themselves. It was a time of fun for our family. We weren't trying to communicate any heavy messages. We were just playing with our kids.

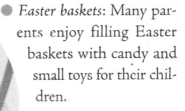

- *Easter baskets*: Many parents enjoy filling Easter baskets with candy and small toys for their children.

- *Easter lilies*: In many churches, Easter lilies are placed in the sanctuary in memory of a loved one. Perhaps your family can contribute a lily in the name of someone you have lost.

- *Hot cross buns*: This is a yummy Easter bread with a white cross on top. For a recipe, see http://www.night.net/easter/recipes.html-ssi.

● *Easter in other lands*: See http://library .thinkquest.org/10007/text/easter .htm.

● *Traditions of Easter*: See http:// wilstar.com/holidays/easter.htm or http://www.oldfashionedliving.com/ eastermem.html.

Thanksgiving

A little more than three hundred years ago, our forefathers stood on the shores of a new land and gave thanks to God for keeping them through the previous year.

Consider all that has happened in the three hundred years since then. Today our land is teeming with people, industry, health facilities, automobiles, homes, and thousands of wonderful things. We have much to thank God for. We should value God's good gifts to us in America. We should teach our children to value them as well. Thanksgiving is a time to do that.

Here are a few celebration ideas.

● Review the story of the Pilgrims by reading a storybook from the library.

138

● A delightful film available on video is *An American Tail*, which tells the story of a Russian mouse family that immigrates to America. At one point, all the mice are pouring onto Ellis Island. In the background, a song can be heard with the words that are engraved on the Statue of Liberty:

Give me your tired, your poor,
Your huddled masses yearning to breathe free,
The wretched refuse of your teeming shore.
Send these, the homeless, tempest-tossed to me,
I lift my lamp beside the golden door.

Emma Lazarus

Although *An American Tail* is a fantasy and not about people, it may help your children understand what it was like for immigrants to come to this country from poverty, oppression, and fear. Talk about it and lead your children in giving thanks for this great land.

● Invite a great-grandparent or a friend who immigrated to the United States to share his or her story with your family. Each person you talk to will have a unique view on what the experience was like.

● Many churches and civic organizations have programs in which volunteers cook and serve dinner to the needy. What a great learning experience it would be for your whole family to be a part of serving the hungry together. Your children will see firsthand that you value people and generosity.

139

- Invite those who have no place to go for Thanksgiving. Every person who sits at your table brings a new insight about life.

Whatever you do, make giving thanks a part of your celebration. If your church has a Thanksgiving Day service, attend it with your children. Talk afterward about how to give thanks to God. Pray together and, by your example, teach your children to offer prayers of thanksgiving to God.

Month-by-Month Celebrations

The following is a list of other celebrations—more time for family fun. Please don't stop with this list. Think of other days and ways you can celebrate life with your children. Make living at your house fun.

January

- *New Year's Day*

For most families, New Year's Day means football, football, and more football. Even if viewing football is to be the order of the day, it is always more fun when family and friends are there to cheer along. Football on television can be a shared experience if dad or mom, whoever is the fan, takes the time to explain to the kids what is happening and to convey his or her love of the game.

● *Martin Luther King Day*

This is an important holiday. Use this day to emphasize the value all people have in God's sight. Your kids need to understand that God loves all people, of all colors and all races. This is a good time to discuss the contribution African-Americans have made to our society.

Because Martin Luther King Jr. is a modern-day hero, it is possible to find a great deal of information about him. Television stations often replay footage of his life, his famous speeches, and his tragic death. You'll find many books about Dr. King in your local library.

Another idea for this day is to use the model of Dr. King's "I have a dream" speech and talk about your family's dream and vision for the future.

● *Snow Day*

If you live in an area where it snows, why not celebrate? Plan a winter picnic with chili in an oversized thermos, sandwiches, hot chocolate, and cookies. Dress warmly, find a sheltered place in the sunshine, and enjoy being together as a family. Play in the snow with the kids, go sledding, or lie in the snow and make snow angels.

■ *February*

● *Groundhog Day*

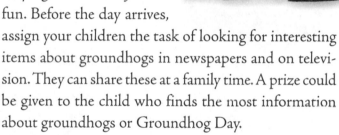

Research the legends associated with this day. Make sure your children understand that they are only legends and are just for fun. Before the day arrives, assign your children the task of looking for interesting items about groundhogs in newspapers and on television. They can share these at a family time. A prize could be given to the child who finds the most information about groundhogs or Groundhog Day.

● *Valentine's Day*

This day is a tribute to Saint Valentine. He was martyred on February 14, AD 270, for refusing to give up Christianity. It is said that Saint Valentine sent a note to a lady friend and signed it "from your Valentine."

The day has been celebrated since the seventh century, and because the day is around the same time birds begin choosing mates, someone decided it would be a good day for young people to choose lovers. Thus the customs relating to hearts, cupids, and love were born.

This holiday is an ideal time to have a special dinner. Flowers and candles make it especially nice. Finish the meal with heart-shaped cookies, a heart-shaped cake, or even a heart-shaped box of candy from the store.

Young children will enjoy making valentines to give to each family member. Older children can help with the meal and dessert.

● *President's Day*

This holiday gives your family a chance to talk about the value of our governmental system. Put up the American flag. Sing patriotic songs. Read a story about George Washington or Abraham Lincoln. Make a recipe from colonial or Civil War times. Here are a few websites with some great recipes: http://www.bownet .org/5ss/colonialrecipes.htm, http://www.history.org/ Almanack/life/food/foodhdr.cfm, and http://www .civilwarindex.homestead.com/RecipeIndex.html.

● *Susan B. Anthony Day*

Find out the contributions Susan B. Anthony made and share this information with your family. If possible, have a Susan B. Anthony dollar to show your children.

March

● *Lion or Lamb Festival*

March is supposed to come in like a blustery, roaring lion and leave like a soft, gentle lamb. Take advantage of the idea and discuss the ways in which Jesus Christ is like a lion or a lamb. Use a concordance to look up references to "lion" or "lamb" in the Bible. You may want to read a passage from The Chronicles of Narnia, in which C. S. Lewis depicts Christ as the lion Aslan.

● *Kite-Flying Festival*

You may want to have your own family kite-flying festival. Real fun can be had with a two-handled kite, which can be made to dip and whirl. You can buy a kite for each person and hook the kites together in a chain. If you haven't visited a kite store lately, you are in for a treat. There you'll find beautiful kites of all shapes and sizes. A good kite will last for years if properly cared for, so it's worth the investment.

● *St. Patrick's Day*

Every year a kind of madness settles in around the middle of March. The madness has a name—"St. Patrick's Day." In some cities with large populations of Irish descendants, the day calls for huge celebrations. Many cities have parades. Chicago dyes the river green. Other cities celebrate with community shows, feasts, and all kinds of exuberant activities.

You can have a lot of fun together as a family on this day. Serve corned beef and cabbage, something green to drink (usually a lime-flavored drink), and something called grasshopper pie, which tastes much better than it sounds. Here is a recipe for grasshopper pie, from the *Calvary Temple, Heaven in the Kitchen Cookbook*:

¼ cup milk
1 7oz. jar marshmallow creme
1 pint whipping cream, whipped
½ tsp. peppermint flavoring
20 Oreo cookies, finely crushed
¼ cup melted butter
   Green food coloring

Mix milk and marshmallow creme until smooth; add to whipped cream. Add peppermint flavoring and green food coloring.

Combine Oreo cookies with melted butter and press into a 9-inch pie pan, saving small amount for top. Pour filling into pan; top with reserved crumbs. Freeze two hours. Serve frozen.

The legends surrounding Saint Patrick, for whom this day was named, are many. Saint Patrick really did exist, and he really did live in Ireland, although he was English. He was captured as a boy by the Irish. After six years, he escaped Ireland, only to return later as a missionary to the Irish people. A series of miracles are said to have occurred when Patrick prayed.

● *First Day of Spring*

> **If ever there was a day to celebrate, it is the coming of spring.**

If ever there was a day to celebrate, it is the coming of spring. Plant some flowers together; go for a walk; find a pond and see if there are any baby ducks or tadpoles yet; go to a park and run; play ball together; or visit a farm to see the new lambs, colts, or calves.

■ *April*

● *April Fool's Day*

Who can start April without at least one prank? Children love to celebrate the day. Help them think up nondestructive pranks to pull on other family members. Let them dress up in polka dots and stripes—anything wild and crazy—and wear funny paper hats at dinner. Play silly, noisy games. Have fun!

● *Arbor Day*

This holiday was traditionally set aside as a day for planting trees. In 1872, long before so many people in the United States became environmentally conscious, a man named Julius Sterling Morton decided that Nebraska would benefit from the wide-scale planting of trees. He set about planting orchards, shade trees, and windbreaks. A few years later, he became a member of Nebraska's State Agricultural Board and proposed setting aside a special day for tree planting.

So, in honor of the tradition, plant a tree. Your children may also learn about this holiday from school. They will be able to teach you what they have learned, or for more info, go to http://www.arbor-day.net/.

● *Time Change—Spring Ahead*

This is the time change we all hate because we have to get up one hour earlier, and it always happens on Sunday. Why not plan a special breakfast and serve it in an unusual spot in the house—like on Mom and Dad's bed, or before a roaring fire, or outside if you live in a warm area? Or perhaps you could take everyone out to breakfast before church.

147

May

● *May Day*

This holiday can be a delightful celebration and a time of giving. Children can make little paper baskets with handles and fill them with garden flowers or little candies. Hang them on the neighbors' doors, then ring the doorbell and run.

● *Mother's Day*

This day is one of the big holidays of the year. Let the children decide what they will do to honor their mother. Dad needs to help make their wishes come true. If they are too young to be aware of how special this day is, he also needs to talk with them about Mother's Day. He needs to help the children find a way to show how much they value their mother.

This can be a tough holiday for single moms. Let the children surprise you, even though you may be aware of what they are planning and even if their plans may result in a messy house. Be truly grateful for their efforts.

148

● *Memorial Day*

This day is for remembering. The apostle Paul encouraged Timothy to remember what he had been taught as a youth. Memorial Day can be a time for remembering those who lived before us. This is a good day to look at old photos and learn more about your family's history. It is also a good time for taking children to visit graves of loved ones and talking about those who've gone to heaven ahead of us.

Many towns have Memorial Day parades with a lot of military activity. Explain what this is all about to your children. Go on a picnic. Spend the day together getting to know one another so that you are building your own memories.

June

● *Flag Day*

This day will be more meaningful to your family if you fly a flag from your house or in your yard. Flag Day is set aside to commemorate the June 14, 1777 adoption by the

149

Continental Congress of a resolution to make the Stars and Stripes the official flag of the United States.

Recite the Pledge of Allegiance together and sing the national anthem. Talk about why we stand at attention when this song is played.

● *Father's Day*

This is Dad's special day. Now it is Mom's privilege to lead her children in honoring their father. Plan a special meal of his favorite foods, serve breakfast in bed, or take him out to eat. Have the children learn a poem or a Scripture verse about fathers and recite it to their dad.

■ *July*

● *Independence Day*

This is the only holiday in July, and it is another good time to fly your American flag. If you allow your children to have their own fireworks, then help them purchase fireworks and supervise their use. Otherwise, you can take your family to your city's fireworks display.

150

Talk about what it means to be a free people and give thanks to God that we are free. Discuss the cost of our freedom and how we can maintain it by being good citizens.

Spend the day with family and friends. Use the time to draw closer together as a family.

■ *August*

● *International Friendship Day*

August is the only month without a traditional holiday, so someone invented International Friendship Day, which is celebrated on August 3. If you have never celebrated this day, then here's your chance. Think of something to do to encourage friendship—having a block party in your neighborhood, sending homemade cards to friends, or letting the children invite a special friend to spend the day or night. Talk together about the value of a good friend.

For more information about this holiday and great ideas on how to celebrate it, visit these websites: http://familycrafts.about.com/cs/augustholidays/l/blaug6th.htm, http://www.friendship.com.au/friendday.html, and http://theholidayspot.com/friendship/.

151

■ *September*

● *Labor Day*

This is the last holiday of summer. Why not do something special, such as a short trip, a picnic, a bike ride, or something you have wanted to do for a long time?

This would be an excellent time to discuss the new school year. You could pray together about your kids' new teachers. You could discuss any fears your kids may be having about the school year ahead. You might even suggest some events or awards for good grades.

● *Grandparents' Day*

This day is celebrated the first Sunday after Labor Day. Help your children think of ways to honor their grandparents. They could call their grandparents and express their love, make or buy a special card, or make a thank-you book and illustrate it themselves. A time of special prayer for grandparents would be appropriate.

● *Beginning of Fall*

Celebrate fall with a leaf-raking-and-burning party, if it is allowed in your area. Go for a walk and kick leaves. Gather colored leaves and award a prize to the person who finds the most beautiful leaf. Pick apples and let the

kids help you make an apple pie. Sit on a hillside and listen to the quiet of an autumn day. Watch for flights of geese and other birds headed south for the winter.

October

● *Columbus Day*

Read together about Christopher Columbus. Trace his route on a world map or globe. Discuss what it would be like to venture to a place where no one from your country has ever been. Compare his journey to that of the first astronauts to the moon. Read in the Bible about Abraham starting off for a country where he had never been. Lead children in talking about trust in God.

Because Columbus was Italian, serve an Italian dinner. Use world maps as place mats and a toy boat for a centerpiece

● *United Nations Day*

Serve an international dinner—first course from one country, main course from another, and so on. Decorate your table with flags from many nations. Put up pictures or posters of cities from other countries.

Talk about how the United Nations was born. Discuss the Scripture verse displayed in the lobby of the UN headquarters: "They shall beat their swords into plowshares, and their spears into pruning hooks; nation shall not lift up sword against nation, neither shall they learn war any more" (Isa. 2:4 RSV).

● *Time Change—Fall Back*

On the last Sunday of October, we turn our clocks back one hour and get some extra sleep. You can have a celebration too. Because everyone can sleep an hour later on Sunday morning, let the children stay up an hour longer on Saturday night and do something together in that extra hour. Read a story, have a pillow fight, go out for hot chocolate, or make popcorn. Talk about time as God's gift and how we need to make the best use of our time. (That includes taking time for fun with our kids.)

Talk about time as God's gift and how we need to make the best use of our time. (That includes taking time for fun with our kids.)

● *Halloween*

When my children were small, not much thought was given to the occult aspect of Halloween. It was sim-

154

ply a fun night for kids to dress up in costumes and go to the neighbors' houses. But today parents need to give some serious thought to this holiday. With so much occult activity and satanic worship in our country and others, we need to be very careful not to open the door to any of this.

And yet, the neighbors' kids are celebrating, and yours will feel bad if they can't. Substitute other activities and do them with such style that not only your kids will want to participate, but the neighbor kids will be asking to come too.

Have an All Saints party where children dress up like a Bible character. Have a harvest festival and visit a pumpkin farm. Eat pumpkin ice cream afterward. Take your kids to the store the day after Halloween and let them buy a generous supply of candy, which will be available at a discounted price.

November

Election Day

Have a red, white, and blue theme at the dinner table. Talk about the responsibility of American citizens to vote. Talk about the relationship between being a good citizen and being a good Christian.

● *Veteran's Day*

This has been a somewhat forgotten holiday in the recent past, but with new wars and new heroes in our faithful armed forces, this day has new meaning. Fly your American flag again today. Talk about the purpose of this day. If you don't know much about the history of this day, visit the following website: http://www1 .va.gov/vetsday/. Research some great American heroes both in the past and in more recent wars. Talk about what these people did for our country.

Discuss people in your family who are veterans. Or better still, if possible, invite those people to come and share their experiences with your children.

■ *December*

● *Bill of Rights Day*

This holiday occurs on December 15. Did you know that such a day exists? The Bill of Rights of the American Constitution is probably the most important document of its kind ever formulated. If your children are old enough, read the Bill of Rights to them and tell them why each point is important. Give them the Christian perspective on each point. For more information, see http://www.holidayorigins.com/html/bill_of_rights_day.html.

● *First Day of Winter*

Have a winter festival. Let your children cut snowflakes from tissue paper and hang them all over your windows. For instructions on how to cut a six-pointed snowflake, see http://www.highhopes.com/snowflakes.html.

Show your children how each paper snowflake is different. Then talk about how God made each snowflake that falls from the sky different from the others.

Let your kids buy new mittens and hats. Buying the apparel could be an outing for the entire family. Make popcorn balls to look like snowballs or pop some corn and string it in preparation for Christmas. Talk about this being the shortest day of the year. Explain how short the days are in places like Alaska and Lapland, which are nearer to the Arctic Circle.

A great website for December holidays is http://www.bry-backmanor.org/holidayfun/dec.html.

Special Occasions

Here are a few more special occasions to celebrate.

● Birthdays: Make the birthday person feel special.

　● First day of school.

　● Last day of school.

　● Anniversaries—parents, grand-parents.

　● Graduation: Fly a banner for the one graduating.

● Special awards won by family members.

● Favorite team wins.

● A special purchase—such as a new car.

● Leaving home—going away to camp, college.

● Coming home again.

How to Save Time for Family Fun

● *Save time by having realistic expectations about housekeeping.* I always laugh at those real-estate ads that say, "Mrs. Clean lives here." I wonder what kind of stress goes on in that household, trying to keep everything clean and in its place all the time. Kids need to be kids, and messes happen when you have kids. If you are trying to be Mrs. Clean, lighten up and enjoy these precious years with your kids. In other words: get real about what's possible when you have an active family.

> **If you are trying to be Mrs. Clean, lighten up and enjoy these precious years with your kids.**

- *Save time by simplifying your lifestyle.* There has been a lot of talk the last few years about simplifying your life. As I look around, I think that's what it's been mostly—talk. But there is a truth here. If you can simplify your life, you can find more time for family fun. A helpful website on this topic is http://www.rightonthemoney.org/shows/116_simplify/.

- *Save time at Christmas—holiday stress relievers.* What can you do with only a few minutes? Here's a starter list. Add to it yourself and post it where you can see it often. When you have a few minutes to kill, pick something off the list and do it. It will help relieve some of your holiday stress by giving you "me time" and saving you from having to do everything at the last minute.

  a. Five minutes:

    Call a friend and schedule a Christmas lunch

Write a thank-you note

Water the Christmas tree

Wrap one gift

Hang some Christmas hand towels in the bathroom

Sign and address three Christmas cards

Tidy the area where your Christmas tree is by sweeping up needles

Hang three Christmas ornaments

b. Ten minutes:

Change the sheets on one of your guest beds (if you are having company)

Fix cups of hot cocoa for you and your kids

Buy a poinsettia

Call for tickets to *A Christmas Carol* or *The Nutcracker*

Read a few pages of a Christmas magazine

Put some evergreen boughs around the house

Put your feet up and look at the tree

Put tinsel on the tree

c. Thirty minutes:

Pick out a present for a friend at the store or online

Check out some books from the library that you have always wanted to read

String some lights on the tree

Read a couple chapters from a book you have always wanted to read

Pick out a special Christmas recipe

Shop for groceries for Christmas dinner

Bake some ready-made Christmas cookies

Wrap yourself up in warm clothes and go for a walk

Snuggle up with your kids and read a Christmas story

$ How to Save Dollars for Family Fun

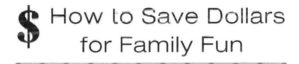

● *Save money on your Christmas tree—a different kind of tree.*

a. Gather pine branches together and put them in a large vase or can decorated with paper. Put water in the vase or can and let the kids decorate to their hearts' delight.

b. Buy a live tree and plant it outside for Christmas. This becomes a living memorial to a Christmas celebration.

c. Find a large, bare branch and pot it in something big enough to support it. Spray paint it white and then add lots of tiny white lights. Let the kids hang their ornaments on it. I guarantee the ornaments will show up better than they would on a green tree.

d. Use a large house plant for a Christmas tree. Decorate it with lights and ribbons.

● *Save money on decorations.* Have you noticed how Christmas comes once a year, every year? So does Independence Day and St. Patrick's Day. If you want to save money on decorations for your home, buy them right after the holiday at a 50 to 75 percent discount and save them for next year. Buy gift wrap and ribbons right after the holidays.

I also watch for gift wrap that could be used for other occasions to go on sale at this time too. Red and white polka dots are not seasonal. Neither is gold or silver paper. So Christmas paper bought in January could be used for someone's birthday in May.

● *Save money on foods and gifts.* Establish a gift shelf or closet in your home. When you see something at a tremendous bargain, buy it and put it on your shelf. Then when you need a gift for a birthday, anniversary, or wedding, you already have it. This saves dollars, and it also saves time since you don't have to go to the store. This year I gave away two china vases I acquired this way. One was Irish porcelain and had a Claddagh, a symbol of friendship, on it. The other vase was a Lenox vase of great charm and value that I was saving for someone very special. I gave it to my brother's new bride.

For most holidays, we want special food, and that special food can be very expensive. Stock up on non-perishable foods when you find them at great savings. Things like nuts, coconut, chocolate chips, and even brown sugar can be frozen and used later. So can big items like turkeys and hams, if you have the room for them in your freezer. Canned goods can include such things as artichoke hearts, maraschino cherries, bacon bits, pickles of all kinds, and lots more favorites. Just don't forget what you have stashed away. A reminder page in your favorite cookbook might be a big help.

"we always"—
the importance
of family traditions

Blessed is the child who grows up in a home where the family has lots of "we always" events. These are the events that happen over and over again. These are the happenings from which vitally important family traditions are built. I say "vitally important" because family traditions give children a unity with and connectedness to something bigger than themselves. Family traditions strengthen not only the family unit but also the individuals within the family by giving them a sense of warmth and emotional closeness. Family traditions provide continuity from one generation to

Family traditions give children a unity with and connectedness to something bigger than themselves.

the next as they help the child feel anchored in his place in the family; he is part of a larger plan—a family plan. Rituals and traditions help families affirm their beliefs and values. "We always" times of going to church together, working in a soup kitchen at Thanksgiving, or recycling for the good of the planet teach children what you value.

Research done at George Washington University's Family Research Center indicates that children fare better in households where tradition is established and preserved. Even if there is a disruptive problem such as divorce or alcoholism in the family, children with traditions still manage better than those who have none. Quiet rituals, such as holding hands while saying a prayer or hearing a story at bedtime, done day after day and year after year, can comfort a child's heart during a stressful time.

Just what constitutes a ritual or a tradition? They are the "we always" events that your family has adopted. The ritual can be something as simple as one person saying "I love you" and the other saying "Love you back," or as complicated as an elaborate holiday meal that is always prepared exactly the same way year after year.

166

A sense of tradition is inherent in Scripture. "The commandments I give you today must be in your hearts. Make sure your children learn them. Talk about them when you are at home. Talk about them when you walk along the road. Speak about them when you go to bed. And speak about them when you get up. Write them down and tie them on your hands as a reminder. Also tie them on your foreheads. Write them on the doorframes of your houses. Also write them on your gates" (Deut. 6:6–9).

This passage of Scripture is a reminder to the Hebrews to pass on the story of how God brought them out of the bondage of Egypt and set them free to be his own children. Do you think only one generation remembering these traditions would be enough? Do you think that's what God intended when he gave the command to teach these truths? No indeed. God intended the Hebrews to establish ritual and tradition in teaching their children about his faithfulness. Passing on stories of faith must continue right down to the present day and in our families. God knows we all need repetition to truly learn.

We read in Psalm 145:4–7, "Parents will praise your works to their children. They will tell about your mighty acts. They will speak about your glorious majesty. . . . They will speak about the powerful and wonderful things you do. . . . They will celebrate your great goodness. They will sing with joy about your holy acts."

Parents, let's praise God for the wonderful tradition of his faithfulness and love that we can hand down to our children. Thank him for the remembrances and rituals, such as baptism and communion, that he commanded us to observe. Rejoice in holidays, such as Christmas and Thanksgiving, when we can celebrate his love for us.

In another Hebrew generation and in a fictional musical, *Fiddler on the Roof*, Tevya, the father of three daughters who are seeking husbands, sings about the importance of tradition to his culture and his family. By listening to the words of his song, we can learn much about when to bend traditions and when bending would destroy something valuable in our families. "On the one hand," says Tevya, "but on the other." There are times when traditions need to be flexed for the good of the family. A time for flexing is when husband and wife are blending the traditions of their two different backgrounds into one. Out of the two traditional backgrounds will come a new tradition that is right for your family and your children. "I cannot bend so far, I will break," Tevya exclaims with fervor. And in your family there are times when unbending tradition is what holds the family together—traditions such as always telling the truth, or in some families, the tradition of doing duty to God and country.

Traditions for Your Family

So what are some ideas for traditions that you can establish for your own family unit? Here is a list.

- Since Sunday is such a special day in the life of a Christian family, make it special.

168

a. Eat breakfast in bed with all the kids there. But what if someone spills? Sheets and blankets are washable, and the fun of all being together is worth a load of wash.

b. Go to church together. And when you get there, as often as possible, sit together.

c. Eat dinner together and sometimes invite company.

d. Have a story hour every Sunday afternoon if your children are small. Make it a ritual.

e. Read the Sunday funnies together.

f. Plan your coming week together.

g. Play a quiet game together.

- Always tell each family member you love him or her before going to bed.

- Schedule a special day on or near a child's birthday in which one or both parents take that child somewhere to honor him or her.

- Celebrate Passover with a Jewish family.

- Bake a traditional food, such as hot cross buns, on Easter.

- Have an un-birthday party on some hot day in August when there are no holidays to celebrate.

- On the longest day of the year, always go for a late-night walk to see the sun go down.

- Always have an extended family picnic or family reunion on the Fourth of July.

- Always have a camping night in your own backyard in summer.

- Make homemade ice cream every Labor Day.

- Always rake big piles of leaves and jump in them in the fall.

- Choose a family activity that is service oriented and do it on a regular basis. It can be a yearly event, like handing out treats at a Christmas party for the elderly, or it can be weekly or monthly, like picking up bulletins after the Sunday service.

- Hold hands when saying grace and always say grace before a meal.

- Always watch a family movie after Thanksgiving dinner, such as *Fiddler on the Roof* (a real sacrifice for the football fans).

- Send out Thanksgiving cards rather than Christmas cards.

- Send out Valentine's Day cards if you missed sending Christmas cards.

- Once a year, have a winter picnic out in the snow with hot soup and hot chocolate from a thermos. Build a huge fire and roast hotdogs or marshmallows.

- Plan an annual Christmas-shopping trip to Wal-Mart or a dollar store and give each child some money to buy presents for everyone. They can make their money go a long way by shopping at a dollar store.

- Always make Christmas cookies.

- Always make a gingerbread house for the Christmas holidays.

- Always have a tree-decorating party and eat the same things for the party year after year.

- Always hang Christmas stockings.

- Always follow a Christmas ritual about gift opening. Make it your family's own tradition.

- Once a year, maybe New Year's Eve, have a family sleepover in the living room.

- Always eat gooey fattening doughnuts on Saturday mornings.

- Always share the best and worst thing that happened to you that day.

- Teach your children about their ethnic background by celebrating your culture's special days.

171

- Always greet each other in the morning, even when a family member feels grumpy.

Plan a Year of Your Own Traditions

So that this concept of having family traditions doesn't just go in one ear (or eye) and out the other, sit down with your family to plan some "we always" events for the upcoming year. Here's a worksheet to help you. Go ahead—write in the book. Then you'll know exactly where to find your plans.

For the "new traditions" section, have your family think up traditions they would like to have in the family. Have your children ask their friends what their families' traditions are. If you like the ideas, incorporate them into your plan. Search some books for little-known events in history that you might want to adopt as traditions for your family. Look into your ethnic background and pull in traditions that will make your children proud of their heritage.

■ *January*

In January, we always:_____

_____

_____

_____

172

These are the traditional calendar holidays in January that we would like to observe: _____

_____

_____

_____

These family members have birthdays in January: _____

_____

_____

_____

For January birthdays, we always: _____

_____

_____

_____

A new tradition we would like to make for January is: ___

_____

_____

_____

The best tradition (new or old) that we have for January is: _____

_____

_____

_____

February

In February, we always: _____
_____
_____
_____

These are the traditional calendar holidays in February that we would like to observe: _____
_____
_____
_____

These family members have birthdays in February: _____
_____
_____
_____
_____

For February birthdays, we always: _____
_____
_____
_____

A new tradition we would like to make for February is:
_____
_____
_____
_____

The best tradition (new or old) that we have for February is: _____

_____

_____

_____

March

In March, we always: _____

_____

_____

_____

These are the traditional calendar holidays in March that we would like to observe: _____

_____

_____

_____

These family members have birthdays in March: _____

_____

_____

_____

For March birthdays, we always: _____

_____

_____

_____

A new tradition we would like to make for March is: ___

_____

_____

_____

The best tradition (new or old) that we have for March is:

_____

_____

_____

_____

April

In April, we always: _____

_____

_____

_____

These are the traditional calendar holidays in April that we would like to observe: _____

_____

_____

_____

These family members have birthdays in April: _____

_____

_____

_____

For April birthdays, we always: _____

_____

_____

_____

A new tradition we would like to make for April is: _____

_____

_____

_____

The best tradition (new or old) that we have for April is:

_____

_____

_____

_____

May

In May, we always: _____   _____

_____

_____

_____

These are the traditional calendar holidays in May that we would like to observe: _____

_____

_____

_____

177

These family members have birthdays in May: _____

_____

_____

_____

_____

For May birthdays, we always: _____

_____

_____

_____

A new tradition we would like to make for May is: _____

_____

_____

_____

The best tradition (new or old) that we have for May is: _

_____

_____

_____

June

In June, we always: _____

_____

_____

_____

These are the traditional calendar holidays in June that we would like to observe: _____

_____

_____

_____

These family members have birthdays in June: _____

_____

_____

_____

For June birthdays, we always: _____

_____

_____

_____

A new tradition we would like to make for June is: _____

_____

_____

_____

The best tradition (new or old) that we have for June is:

_____

_____

_____

July

In July, we always: _____

_____

_____

_____

These are the traditional calendar holidays in July that we would like to observe: _____

_____

_____

_____

_____

These family members have birthdays in July: _____

_____

_____

_____

For July birthdays, we always: _____

_____

_____

_____

_____

A new tradition we would like to make for July is: _____

_____

_____

_____

The best tradition (new or old) that we have for July is: __

_____

_____

_____

August

In August, we always: _____

_____

_____

_____

These are the traditional calendar holidays in August that we would like to observe: _____

_____

_____

_____

_____

These family members have birthdays in August: _____

_____

_____

_____

For August birthdays, we always: _____

_____

_____

_____

A new tradition we would like to make for August is: ___

_____

_____

_____

_____

The best tradition (new or old) that we have for August is:

_____

_____

_____

_____

September

In September, we always: _____

_____

_____

_____

These are the traditional calendar holidays in September that we would like to observe: _____

_____

_____

_____

These family members have birthdays in September:

_____

_____

_____

_____

For September birthdays, we always: _____

_____

_____

_____

A new tradition we would like to make for September is:

_____

_____

_____

_____

The best tradition (new or old) that we have for September is: _____

_____

_____

_____

October

In October, we always: _____

_____

_____

These are the traditional calendar holidays in October that we would like to observe: _____

_____

_____

These family members have birthdays in October: _____

_____

_____

_____

For October birthdays, we always: _____

_____

_____

_____

A new tradition we would like to make for October is:

_____

_____

_____

_____

The best tradition (new or old) that we have for October is:

_____

_____

_____

_____

November

In November, we always: _____

_____

_____

_____

These are the traditional calendar holidays in November that we would like to observe: _____

_____

_____

_____

These family members have birthdays in November: ___

_____

_____

_____

_____

For November birthdays, we always: _____

_____

_____

_____

A new tradition we would like to make for November is:

_____

_____

_____

The best tradition (new or old) that we have for November is:

_____

_____

_____

_____

December

In December, we always: _____

_____

_____

185

These are the traditional calendar holidays in December that we would like to observe: _____

_____

_____

_____

These family members have birthdays in December: ____

_____

_____

_____

For December birthdays, we always: _____

_____

_____

_____

A new tradition we would like to make for December is:

_____

_____

_____

_____

The best tradition (new or old) that we have for December is: _____

_____

_____

_____

⧖ How to Save Time for Family Fun

Have you ever heard "But I need it tomorrow" from a child at 8:30 p.m.? It doesn't matter what it is they need "tomorrow" or what action you decide to take with regard to the situation, your child's words instantly create family tension. Here are some tips that will not only save time but help to reduce the tension surrounding the announcement.

● *Find out when the child comes home from school* exactly what homework he has and if there are any "projects" looming on the horizon.

● *Purchase some basic tools to help with homework.* Today, a home computer with Internet service can provide all the tools your child needs. Consider investing in a computer and Internet service if you do not already have them. Then understand that you will need to monitor your child's use of the Internet.

● *Keep a supply of supplies.* The Internet is great, but when a child needs glue and paper and other creative items, a computer cannot provide them. You can save yourself a lot of time if you keep on hand a supply of colored construction paper, felt-tipped pens, other writing tools, paper clips, adhesive tapes of various kinds, hole punches, file cards, folders and binders, glue, and other supplies. Having such a stock will avoid quick trips to

187

the drug store or supermarket to try to find these items late at night.

- *Keep a costume trunk.* Nothing is worse for a parent than the announcement that a child needs a costume the next day—especially if that announcement comes late in the day. A costume trunk is also great fun to have around for impromptu plays your kids could be encouraged to give.

- *Keep your own reference file of photos and pictures that can be incorporated into reports.* Yes, a child can get anything she needs from the Internet, but it is still good to have a file of information in hard-copy format to incorporate into reports. Clip interesting information from magazines and newspapers as "starter" ideas for kids' reports.

- *Plan ahead.* Talk with teachers in conferences about what reports and projects are expected in the next few months. As much as possible, nail down a date so that you can be ready for your child's request for materials and help.

$ How to Save Dollars for Family Fun

If you have filled out the family traditions planning tool in this chapter, most of your planning is already done for the year. If you know, for example, that every year on the Fourth of July your family goes on a hot dog roast on the beach with a hundred cousins, you know you will need lots of hot dogs, buns, mustard, catsup, and relish. Watch for sales on these items and buy them ahead of time. Freeze the hot dog buns and hot dogs and don't open the jars of condiments. You can buy the hot dogs six months out, the bread up to six weeks ahead of time, and the condiments at the end of the summer at great savings.

part III
getting out and about as a family

a night on the town— more than movies

In some families, children grow up without going to see even one art show or traveling exhibit because it is not something their parents enjoy. That's all right. Each family enjoys and values different kinds of activities. Different is not wrong; it's just different. Many families enjoy sporting events above cultural events. That's all right. But being exposed to cultural events in addition to sporting events stretches our children and gives them a broader view of the world. This is something worth considering when deciding how your family's limited entertainment budget will be spent.

Any metropolitan area offers more cultural events than you can possibly find time to attend. Even if you do not live in a metropolitan area, you can still find cultural events locally.

Take, for example, a small town in Arkansas, deep in the heart of middle America. One would not expect to find much going on there. But posted on this town's website was something called "Heritage Month" in which the town celebrates its history. Included in the free cultural events for this small town were

- Heritage Day, with a parade and lots of live music. The local heritage museum was open extra hours with special exhibits including a Native American cultural display
- Civil War reenactments
- A storytelling session to celebrate Hispanic contributions to Arkansas' heritage
- A photo display at the railroad museum showing railroad activities throughout Arkansas towns

In addition to these events, the site listed dozens of small towns in the surrounding area, each celebrating its heritage as well.

The point is that even if your town is small, remember children learn best by experience. They will never forget a Civil War reenactment. The War Between the States becomes living history for them. Teach your kids to value cultural events. They will be the recipients of a wonderful legacy of learning that they cannot get any other way.

You can find out what your town offers by visiting its website. Just go to a search engine such as Google, type in the town's name, and see what pops up. If you don't have Internet access, watch the weekend papers for upcoming events. Even if you do have Internet access, you might still want to watch the events section of your paper, as the information is often more current than that found on websites.

Some Cultural Events to Consider

Symphony

Going to a symphony doesn't have to mean hours and hours of baroque music. Today's symphonies, in an effort to lure people back to the events, have done some pretty amazing things. Some symphony events are held outdoors during the summer months. One of my favorite events is a Fourth of July celebration held at Greenfield

195

Village near Detroit, complete with cannons firing to the *1812 Overture* and fireworks at the conclusion of the evening. Other symphonies have laser shows to accompany the music, and some have actors and dancers participating. Some play to child-friendly themes: cartoon sound tracks, television tunes and jingles, and Disney movies tunes. Look for performances that are kid friendly.

Going to a symphony doesn't have to mean hours and hours of baroque music.

Even if you cannot take your family to a symphony, consider introducing them to classical music. Did you know researchers have proven that children who listen to classical music perform better on standardized achievement tests, and children learn to read faster when lessons are accompanied by classics? Did you know that children with problems such as ADD and other learning disabilities learn better when there is classical music in their lives? Did you know that learning music gives at-risk kids more confidence in their ability to succeed at positive activities, rather than those that are destructive to themselves and others? If you can't go to a concert, at

196

least have classical music in your home. Classical music is great background for a nap.

▇ Ballet

Ballet is more than people wearing tights and tutus and jumping around on a stage. First of all, ballet is an athletic event requiring great physical discipline and strength training. Second, it is a story told in dance. And third, it is simply a beautiful thing to behold, with costumes and scenery and a kind of magic. At least once in your children's lives, take them to see a ballet. We've already mentioned in another chapter that *The Nutcracker Suite* is an excellent introduction to ballet. So is *Swan Lake.*

▇ Plays

There are a number of cities that have summer theater in the park. Presentations are chosen with family viewing in mind. I once saw *Cyrano De Bergerac* in a park in my little hometown in Montana, of all places. I've seen Shakespeare outdoors in Fort Worth and Seattle and at

197

the Shakespearean Festival in Ashland, Oregon. See what kinds of theater in your area are kid friendly and fun for the whole family. You might have to plan your theater-going event for the Christmas or other holiday season to find appropriate material for the whole family.

■ Opera

At least once, consider taking your children to see an opera. Before going, make sure every member of the family understands the story being told musically. Even if the opera is in English, get a copy of the story and talk about it together.

> **At least once, consider taking your children to see an opera.**

■ Museums

When it comes to cultural events and destinations, don't neglect taking your family to museums. Go to small-town museums where your children will not be overwhelmed by the amount of artifacts on display and the theme of the museum is more focused. Go to city museums but don't try to take in the whole museum in one day. At some point in your children's lives, try to get them to the Smithsonian Institution in Washington DC, the Museum of Natural History and the Museum of Science and Industry in Chicago, or the de Young Museum in San Francisco. There is a wealth of information that embeds itself so much better if the child sees and hears it at a museum. When your child has seen Thomas Edison's laboratory reconstructed at Greenfield Village in Dearborn, Michigan, he will understand the sacrifice of time and energy Edison put into developing something we take for granted every day—the lightbulb.

■ *Art Galleries*

Most art galleries, unless they are very small and specialized, have something for everyone. Art galleries have not only paintings, but reconstructed rooms of ancient houses and castles. Some have costumes and personal ornamentation displays. Others specialize in Oriental art objects and porcelains. In an art gallery, you will find sculpted figures, some from marble and others cast in bronze. If you can, let them see the brilliant blues of a Van Gogh, the lacy collars and cuffs of a Rembrandt, and the strange, distorted view of a Picasso.

If your art gallery offers cassette recorders, rent them for your family to use as you walk through the displays. The tape will have comments and information on the displays that may be unavailable from other sources. Remember, in either museums or art galleries, take the experience in bite-sized pieces. The brain can only absorb so much information. If the gallery is in your hometown or in a nearby town, plan to make several trips there to enjoy the art. Don't try to do it all in one excursion.

■ Traveling Exhibits

When my children were small, we visited a traveling exhibit of King Tut artifacts. Of all the special exhibits we saw during the children's growing-up years, I believe King Tut, with all its opulence, was our favorite. But there were other memorable traveling exhibits as well.

● *Fabergé eggs.* These exquisite art objects were made for the family of Czar Nicolas of Russia. The eggs are encrusted with gems and gold. Some have tiny doors that open to miniature scenes. One has a huge emerald set at the top. Others have mechanical parts or have scenes painted all the way around the outside of the egg.

● *The treasures of imperial China.* I saw this unexpected and delightful exhibit in a small museum in Santa Ana, California. Among the items of greatest interest to me was a scale model of the Imperial Palace, complete in every detail. Also on display were the quilted soldiers' uniforms of various eras, headdresses for various periods of Chinese history, and beautifully carved jade pieces. But the most fascinating were the royal silk gowns that had been hand embroidered in silken thread. Among the royal vestments was the coronation costume for the last emperor of China. He was less than three years old when crowned. The tiny garment was exquisitely made and worthy of a ruler, even if that ruler were only two and a half years old.

- *Dead Sea Scrolls.* One never knows where these traveling exhibits will turn up. I saw the Dead Sea Scrolls in Grand Rapids, Michigan. While these fragmented scraps of ancient scrolls are not particularly beautiful to look at, just to be near something so old and so important to our faith was thrilling.

▊ *Sporting Events*

Attending these can cost a lot of money, but if your family values the determination, competition, training, and skills of athletes, then make sporting events a high priority on your "night out" activity list. Once in a while (perhaps for a special event like straight As or someone's birthday), go ahead and spend the big bucks for tickets to an NFL, NBA, or NHL game or other sporting event. Just once our kids got to see a national ice-skating competition. We had been watching the ice skaters on television for years, and it was wonderful to see them in person.

After attending one of these sporting events, talk with your kids about the commitment it takes to make something look so effortless. Find out what their goals are and what kind of a commitment it would take to reach those goals. And don't forget local sports events. Every town in America has some kind of sporting program. There are local swim meets, Little League baseball, high school and college basketball and football games, volleyball tournaments, tennis matches, and on and on. These are inexpensive and fun for families.

■ *Dinner Out*

If you can possibly squeeze it into your budget, take your kids out to eat occasionally at a nice restaurant. Teach them which fork to use and when. Then later in life when they are confronted by an array of silverware at some formal dinner, they will not be intimidated or feel ill at ease. Give them the social skills they will need, so that when your parenting tasks are done, your children will be equipped for life.

Eating out can be an ethnic adventure. You can eat borscht in a Russian restaurant, curry in an East Indian restaurant, or goat in an African restaurant. Go to English high tea in a fancy hotel or order souvlaki in a Greek restaurant. Give your children a wide variety of food experiences. In doing so, you are exposing them to a broader view of life and creating patterns of interest that will expand them as people. You too will grow as a person as you share these adventures with your children.

⌛ How to Save Time for Family Fun

Barter for more time. That means swapping something you know how to do for something you don't with neighbors and friends. Can you do accounting, but not gardening? Swap to save both time and money.

Exchange child care. Ever tried to paint with a two-year-old underfoot? If you haven't tried it, don't. Here's a good time to get help from a friend in exchange for babysitting sometime when she needs a block of time.

Hire a housecleaner. If you can afford it, this is a great way to get more time in your life. You can have a housecleaner come either weekly or only occasionally for deep cleaning. Housecleaners come to clean the house and not to pick up after your kids, so teach your kids to hang up clothes, put soiled clothing in the laundry basket, and pick up all their toys so the housecleaner can find the floor to clean it.

Teach your kids to work. Here's a novel idea. If you think it's faster to do something yourself rather than ask your kids to do it, think again. It may be true that it takes more time while kids are in training on a task. But if you hang in there, children can truly learn to work in a way that helps rather than hinders. When they are able to work well, it will not only save on the time you have to work, but it will save you hiring someone else to do the work. And it will teach your children the value of work and the satisfaction of a job well done.

If you are going to teach your child to work, you must step back and think about what you understood about work at his age. Did you have any idea how to clean a bedroom? Or wash a car? Or weed a flower bed? Begin at that point. Cut a large, complex task apart into bite-sized pieces and begin by teaching the way to do each bite-sized piece. For example, if you send a child to clean his room, he may be overwhelmed and do nothing. But if you work with him and train him as you go, he has a chance at success. A workable dialogue might be, "First we have to get everything off the floor so we

204

can clean. Let's pick up all the toys and put them where they belong." Give the child the opportunity to do that. "Good," you might say, "that looks better already. Now let's pick up all the clothes and hang them up." (We'll assume the hooks and clothes rods are at the right height for the child to reach.) Then you can say, "Now that we have everything put away, we can go on. Here's a dust cloth, and this is how we use it." Show the child how to dust the furniture. Show him how to make the bed. Decide whether or not she is big enough to handle the vacuum cleaner and if so, show her how to use it.

> Cut a large, complex task apart into bite-sized pieces and begin by teaching the way to do each bite-sized piece.

Every job you give a child should have a beginning and an end. It should be short enough to be within her attention span. Sometimes a little challenge helps to motivate the child. How much do you think you can get done in the next five minutes? Can you clean your whole room in half an hour? When the task is finished, congratulate the child. If you want children to try again, they need encouragement.

Hire your children. Kids should have some jobs they do just because they live in the home. There are other tasks, however, such as yard work, washing windows, and washing cars, that they can be paid to do. When my son was a teenager, I paid

205

him to vacuum for me. It was a task I not only didn't like, but never seemed to get to. For all of us, money is a good incentive to work. And when you pay your own children, you save both time and money as the money stays in the family.

$ How to Save Dollars for Family Fun

- *Plays.* To save money, go to local events. High school and college plays are performed well and are lots of fun. Civic theater is fresh, innovative, and fun. It is also inexpensive.

- *Symphony and other musical events.* Get a season pass for your family. It's cheaper than individual tickets. Go to a local college concert. It will probably be free. Watch for summertime outdoor performances by local musical groups.

- *Volunteer.* Volunteers often get free passes after they do so many hours of volunteer labor. You can use these passes for any member of your family.

- *Half-price tickets.* Buy tickets at half price the day of the show. Find where these ticket outlets are in your city.

- *Rush tickets.* Buy tickets minutes before the show for the best bargains. These are called "rush" tickets. They go on sale at the box office about twenty to thirty minutes before the event begins. But don't count on getting the tickets. If this is to be a family event, you'd better have a back-up plan.

- *Classified ads.* Often season-ticket holders can't attend all of their shows and may sell single-event tickets for a particular performance at a discount.

- *Free tickets.* Let your friends and business associates know which events your family likes to attend. They may give you tickets to events. I once had the privilege of attending a U.S. Air Force football game with fifty-yard-line seats because a neighbor knew I wanted to go and take my parents. Also, check with your company and let them know what events you like to attend. Organizations give corporations blocks of tickets for sporting events, the theater, and the symphony.

- *Free days.* Many art museums have a free day each week, or for some, once a month. Check their websites or call to find out when it is.

- *Outdoor art festivals.* These are free.

- *"Freebies for families."* Type that title into a search site on the Internet for free gifts of all kinds.

the ultimate out-and-about adventure— the family vacation

Vacation? Who needs a vacation? Who needs the hassle, the upset stomachs, the fighting in the backseat of the car? The expense?

Ever heard that kind of talk? Well, the truth is that *everyone* needs a vacation. Everyone needs to get away from routine and do something completely different for a while. It is essential that we get away from responsibilities, telephones, and schedules sometime during the year. Vacations are a wonderful way to get to know our kids better. Sitting around a pool somewhere, you might find out what's really going on in their heads. When there is an argument about where to go next or what to do next, you have a wonderful opportunity to teach problem-solving and people-management skills.

But the truth is that for some families, vacation time can also be a time of great stress. Most families are not used to being shut up together for days on end. However, some of the stress related to family vacationing can be reduced by good planning and a realistic approach to your time away. Today there are hundreds (maybe even thousands) of websites to help you build a wonderful vacation and save money doing it.

Reduce Expectations

One thing you can do to reduce the stress of a family vacation is to lower your expectations. Families who intend to drive three thousand miles in three weeks have no time for relaxation, and after a while, no one cares what you are seeing or learning along the way. Kids and parents alike just want to go home.

So first of all, understand what a vacation is about. It is a time of "re-creation," a time to "re-create" yourself. It is a time

210

to rest, a time to read a book that is not required reading, a time to sleep in or to stay up late, whichever suits you best. It's a time for seeing some new sights. It's a time for reflection and talk that could include parents, kids, and grandparents. It's a time for talking about family values and asking each other the hard questions of life.

If you want to go somewhere, say to another state, why don't you try meandering your way there rather than racing to your destination? One of the best vacations I ever had was not to another state, but to another country—Ireland. And one of the reasons it was great was that all the travel brochures warned against trying to make more than one hundred miles a day. So I heeded the advice. I took Ireland in bite-sized pieces, and if I came to a town that had particular appeal, I spent some time there, perhaps even staying overnight at a B&B. I made it a practice to find a place to stay for the night by about four in the afternoon. Knowing I'd have a bed and a roof over my head reduced my stress. I would have dinner and walk around the town to see what there was to see; then I would go back to the B&B to read for a while or sit chatting with the host. It was wonderful.

Is having no reservations practical for a family that is traveling at the height of tourist season? Perhaps there needs to be a

Don't try to do too much or go too far. Leave time for discovering new things along the way.

little more structure as to where you will stay. No one wants to spend the night in a car. But the point is, don't try to do too much or go too far. Leave time for discovering new things along the way. Leave time for fully investigating a new place. If you stop at an outdoor museum—say a reconstructed fort—and your kids are having a ball, let them stay till they are done playing. They will be satisfied with the experience, and they will never forget it.

Planning Ahead

Planning makes the difference. So where do we start?

If your family has never taken the time to sit down together and decide where you would like to travel, make planning your first task. Let's talk about how to get a plan.

■ Set Goals for Family Travel

1. Do "green-light brainstorming." Green-light brainstorming simply means that all systems are go. Anyone can propose anything as a vacation possibility, with no censoring. Maybe as the parent, you think what is suggested is too expensive or too lofty or too impossible a dream, but you don't know that for sure. Anything is possible.

2. Write down every idea on a big card (or an 8½ x 11 sheet of paper). Tape these cards or sheets on the wall.

3. When everyone has exhausted every possible idea for vacation spots, then together determine which should be long vacations and which could be done as extended weekend trips. Move the cards into two columns: short vacations and long vacations.

4. Now, look at the long vacations and decide which one your family wants to do first, second, etc. Number the cards in order of vacation preference and tape them in that order. Do the same with the weekend trips.

5. Pick the first card—the family's number-one-priority long vacation. Let's see how you could make that vacation happen.

◾ Decide What It Would Take to Make This #1 Vacation Happen

1. Finances. There is always the problem of finances, so first you have to determine if your family can afford the hoped-for vacation. Someone—usually the person who takes care of the finances—must figure out where the money will come from. If your children are older, let them help with the financial side of planning for a vacation.

2. Coordinate schedules. This is an easy one when the kids are small. If both parents are employed, they simply put in for the time they want off and wait to have it approved. But if your children are older and have jobs or multiple activities, then everyone must arrange

213

a vacation time. Start with a couple of suggested times for your vacation. Alternate times will only be a problem if your destination is an event, such as a family wedding.

3. Collect information. Assign someone to start collecting information about your destination, planning a route, and finding out what interesting sites are on the way to your destination. Perhaps these tasks could be divided up between the Internet geniuses that live at your house.

4. Choose lodgings. When a route has been chosen and some semblance of an easygoing schedule has been established, assign one member to look for lodging in the right town, for the right night, for the right dollars. Have the researcher print out all the information and then get the family together for a final before-we-book planning session.

Nothing ensures a perfect vacation, but with this much involvement from your entire family, you and your children should be anticipating a great time together.

Inexpensive Vacations

I have been accused of being a genius at finding travel bargains. That trip I took to Ireland? It cost me about $1000 for ten days, including two days in London where you can

214

drop a twenty-dollar bill every hour. How did I take a trip like that for so little money?

- *Airline miles.* First of all, I accumulated airline miles for the flight portion of the trip. It took a few years to get enough, but eventually I had them.

- *Booked accommodations and car ahead.* I booked a tour that included a car and vouchers for five nights of B&Bs. A book listing bed and breakfasts all over Ireland came with the package, so it was easy to find a place to stay. Because I didn't have a roommate, I had to pay a little more to have single room occupancy, but even that didn't add a lot to the total.

- *Saved on food.* All the accommodations came with a hefty breakfast, and I ate it all. My noon meal usually came from a small café or was fruit and cheese that I bought in a shop. I really wasn't very hungry after that big breakfast, and I was looking forward to an evening meal in the town where I was staying. My B&B host always knew where to send me for dinner. So the only expense worth talking about for food for the day was the evening meal. Sometimes I ate that meal in an Irish pub, sometimes in a regular restaurant. Pub food is hot and nourishing and inexpensive. Pubs are where Irish families gather in the evenings. Some were a little smoky, but not much more than the restaurants. There's usually music and a lot of talking and laughing. If you really want to know the Irish people, you must at least visit a pub.

215

You can find travel bargains by signing up for online travel notification from companies such as Travelocity, Expedia, Orbitz, Hotwire, and Priceline. And you can sign up for notification about travel to select destinations. For example, because my son and his family are in Boston, I want to know when a great fare to Boston shows up. I am notified automatically by several of these sites. Here are some other ways to get good deals.

- Sign up for airline hot deals. Many airlines have complete packages for tourist destinations and international travel that are unbelievably inexpensive. They too will notify you of a favorite destination.

- Move quickly when a great fare shows up. They can sell out in minutes, so be ready to move.

- Be flexible in your travel schedule. Most of these sites have a flexible-schedule feature that will save you the most money. If you click into that web page, you will see a calendar noting which days have the best fares. Follow the directions and be amazed at the great fares you can get by being flexible. Sometimes this just won't work with your schedule, but it's worth a try.

- Make more than one connection. If you can stand to do this, you might find fares reduced even further.

- Look for special discounts at these travel sites for grandparents age sixty-five and over.

- Travel on the train for a great experience and reasonable fares.

- Travel by bus. There are places you can reach only this way.

- Use the sites listed above to search for rental cars, hotels, etc. Priceline is great for hotels. I've stayed in three- and four-star hotels for less than fifty dollars per night. I've also stayed in two-star hotels for about twenty-five dollars per night.

Packing

The cardinal rule is: DON'T TAKE TOO MUCH! I don't know whether it was having young children and all their stuff that cured me of taking more than I need on a trip; or the incessant travel I did when I was an acquisitions editor; or the fact that I usually pack my books, and if there is any space left, I put some clothing into the suitcase. (It's not quite that bad, but almost.)

Just remember when you are considering whether to tuck in one more pair of shoes, one more jacket, or one more bulky sweater: you are the one who will lift and carry your suitcases. How much stuff do you want to physically move? Remember, more stuff means more weight, and more weight means you have to lug it, lift it, and drag it.

If in your attempt to cut down weight and bulk, you don't take enough of something, you have a wonderful excuse for buying something you truly *need*.

■ What Clothes Should We Take?

Rule number 1: Take only what you need.

The answer to having what you need and only what you need for either a weekend family adventure or an extended vacation lies in planning.

The answer to having what you need and only what you need for either a weekend family adventure or an extended vacation lies in planning, and the chart on page 221 makes planning a breeze. I was recently with a friend who travels and speaks for a living. She was groaning about packing and not knowing what to take. I pushed this chart in front of her. She filled it out quickly, and the packing was done within minutes. Planning ahead using the chart lets you know what you will wear when, and it assures you that everything you need to make the outfit complete is with you.

218

Rule number 2: Pick one basic color scheme for everything you take on the trip.

For summer vacations, it will probably be blue denim or khaki shorts and pants. For Mom it might be navy blue skirts, shorts, and pants. When you pick the tops (T-shirts and other shirts), plan so everything you take coordinates with all the other pieces. For example, if you choose navy blue as your basic color, start with one navy blue skirt and a couple of navy blue pants or shorts. Add two or three tops. They can be red, beige, white, and any pattern that coordinates with navy blue. Black would not coordinate, so leave shirts and tops with black in them at home.

Rule number 3: Make sure every family member takes a white T-shirt.

White T-shirts go with everything. They can be used for sleeping. You can stuff them with clothes to make a pillow if the one provided is too hard. You can wear a white T-shirt as a beach cover-up to avoid sunburn. If you need to dress up, you can tuck the T-shirt in and add a jacket or blazer, and you are ready for a dressier occasion. If the T-shirt gets really grimy, an all-white T-shirt is easy to bleach white again.

Rule number 4: Plan to wash clothes when traveling.

This rule makes not taking too much possible. It's not difficult to find a washing facility wherever you are. Many hotels now offer coin-operated laundry facilities for guests. If you are on a ten-day vacation, plan to wash clothes about halfway through the trip, so take clothes for six days and you'll have a set to wear while your other clothes are being washed.

Fewer is better, so perhaps you can find a way to cut down even more on the amount of clothes you take.

Here's how to use the chart.

1. Make a chart for each person or let everyone make their own.

2. In the "Date" column, write the date or day of the week—Monday, Tuesday, or 10/12, 10/13.

3. In the "Bottom" column, write the skirt, shorts, or pants you or a family member will wear that day.

4. In the "Top" column, write the top—blouse, jacket, sweatshirt, tank top, T-shirt, or other top—you will wear with the skirt, shorts, or pants you have chosen.

5. Under "Shoes," write the footwear appropriate to this outfit. Limit the pairs of shoes you take as they add considerable weight to your luggage. Try to take only one pair of sport or walking shoes and one pair of dress shoes, sandals, or whatever is appropriate for your trip. Use your socks for slippers or take fold-up slippers or flip-flops.

6. Under "Socks," write the type you need for the outfit you've chosen. (For example, if you are dressing up during a trip, women will probably need to include panty hose, and men will need dress socks.)

7. Under "Accessories," write down the hats, scarves, ties, jewelry, etc. you will need for the day.

Date	Bottom	Top	Shoes	Socks	Underclothes	Accessories

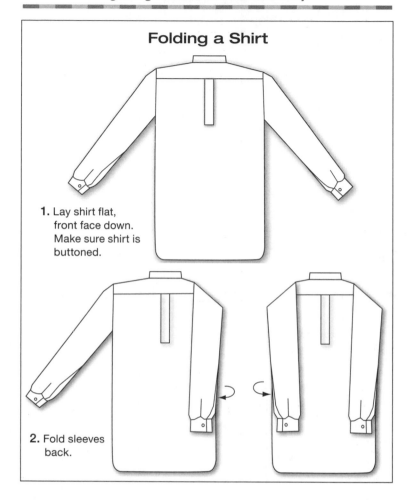

Folding a Shirt

1. Lay shirt flat, front face down. Make sure shirt is buttoned.

2. Fold sleeves back.

■ *Packing It in the Suitcase*

1. Pile all the clothing going into one family member's suitcase on the bed.

2. Fold the heaviest items and put them in first. Jeans, pants, and sweaters make a good base for the rest of your packing.

222

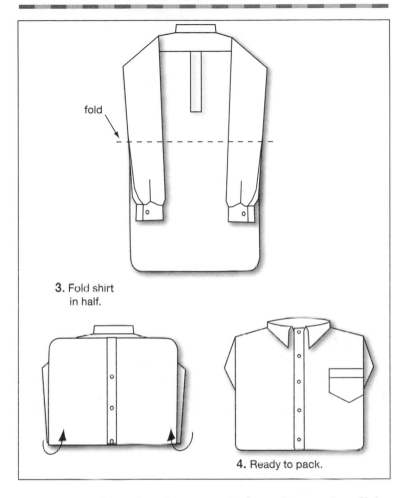

3. Fold shirt in half.

4. Ready to pack.

3. Put socks and underwear in lock-top bags and stuff the bags into the shoes.

4. Place the stuffed shoes along the back of the suitcase when it is in its upright position.

5. If you are taking skirts, fold them the least amount of times necessary to get them into the suitcase. Straight skirts travel best.

223

6. Fold underwear, pajamas, and swimsuits and put them in next.

7. Fold blouses, shirts, and T-shirts, as shown on the previous pages, and put them in next.

8. Stuff small items, such as accessories, into the corners of your suitcase.

9. Do not pack valuables in any bag that will be checked.

10. If you are packing, rather than wearing, your raincoat, fold it and put it on top where you can get to it if there is a sudden shower.

11. Put an umbrella in an outside pocket.

12. Keep all prescription medications in your carry-on bag.

I've tried a lot of devices for packing cosmetics, but the cosmetic kit I like best is the kind you can hang up. It has clear pockets with zippers. When fully packed and hung on the bathroom door at your hotel, it's like having your own medicine cabinet with you. These cases fold in thirds and fit right into your suitcase. However, I usually put my cosmetic kit, which might also have medications in it, in my carry-on luggage.

When everything is inside the suitcase, fasten the elastic straps provided to keep things from shifting and wrinkling.

The Trip Back

If you are concerned that you won't have enough space for things you'd like to bring back from a trip, especially a vacation abroad where you plan to shop, there are several things you can do.

- *Ship purchases home.* While you have to pay for shipping, it can actually be to your advantage to ship since you will not have to pay Value Added Tax (VAT) on those goods.

- *Bring a folded canvas bag with strong handles.* Put it flat in the very bottom of your suitcase, never to be unpacked unless you need it. I collect free canvas bags wherever I can. If I don't use them, I can always give them to a traveling companion who has overloaded a suitcase. Mesh or string bags are great because you can tuck them into corners of a suitcase. Once in use, they have great expansion capacity. Once in a while I get caught without a canvas bag, or the one I brought isn't big enough, so I stop by a local thrift shop and buy what I need. The last bag I bought was a canvas duffle with fun designs on it made by The Gap. It cost me twenty-five

225

cents. I checked it right along with the rest of my luggage and gave it away after the trip.

Travel Tips

- When staying in B&Bs that have communal baths, instead of taking a bulky bathrobe, use your raincoat for a cover-up. It's lightweight, packs small, and, of course, can be worn as a raincoat. If you have a private bath, you don't need a robe at all.

- Wear your heaviest clothing while traveling. This will save lots of space in your luggage.

- Ladies, by color-coordinating your wardrobe, you will need only one set of cosmetics and jewelry, so don't take more.

- Purchase a small, folding hair dryer if you think you'll need one at all. Many accommodations now provide hair dryers, so check with your hotel or B&B to see if it does.

- Take along a genuine wool sweater if you think there is any chance of cool weather or for warding off chills from air conditioning. A wool sweater under a good waterproof raincoat will keep you warm unless the temperature is quite cold. While you hope to stay dry, even wet wool has warming capabilities. Pick a sweater that coordinates with the rest of the clothing you have chosen for your trip.

● If you travel often, get yourself a travel alarm clock. Some have flashlights built in; others come with an AM/FM radio. Some have dual time zone information.

Preparing Your Home
for Your Absence

Here is a ten-point checklist for leaving your home.

1. Stop mail and newspaper delivery. Ask delivery services like UPS and FedEx to hold deliveries until notified.

2. To deter burglars, trim the bushes so your house is very visible from the street.

3. Don't provide any extra details on your answering machine. Just have a generic message such as "we can't come to the phone right now."

4. Use timers to turn several lights throughout the house on and off. If possible, place at least one outside light on a timer as well. Leave draperies open a bit, especially on upper-level floors that aren't easily visible.

5. Make sure the lights on those automatic timers are working. Replace any bulbs that are burned out.

6. Don't make it easy for burglars. Make sure all windows are intact and working well. Install deadbolts if you

haven't already. Take in hidden keys. Take in garage-door openers from cars that might be parked outside.

7. Let a neighbor you trust know you will be away and have them hold a spare key. If you have a "neighborhood watch," let them know you are away. In a more remote area, you might want to notify law enforcement agencies of your absence.

8. Turn off the water main to make sure there are not unattended water leaks.

9. Prepay bills—it won't do much for household safety, but it will allow you to enjoy your vacation more fully.

10. Make arrangements for your pets and plants to be cared for in your absence.

Travel Books to Help You

● For new Internet users, read *e-Travel*, published by SAMS, www.samspublishing.com (ISBN 0–672–31822–9).

● Traveling with an infant or small child brings up a new set of problems. Fodor has published *Travel with Your Baby* (ISBN 0–676–90134–4).

● For grandma, read *More Women Travel*, published by Rough Guides (ISBN 1–85828–098–2).

● For older adults, there is *Gypsying After 40*, published by John Muir Publications, Inc. (ISBN 0–912528–71–0).

How to Save Time for Family Fun

Save time by using the packing checklist below.

____ Clothing—use the chart on page 221

____ Underwear—take six underpants, two bras, and a half-slip for the ladies in the family and six underpants for the men (and six undershirts if your men wear them). You'll only have to wash them once during a twelve-day trip

____ Cosmetics—in a travel case

____ Medications and vitamins—in small, lock-top plastic bags, one for each day

____ Hair dryer, curling iron—fold-up and in travel case if possible

____ Outerwear—raincoat and fold-up umbrella

____ Wool sweater unless you know it's going to be very hot—then take a lightweight sweater or shawl for protection against air-conditioning chills

____ Small pillow—make a dark-colored pillowcase with handles. It won't show dirt or makeup. The handles make it possible to carry the pillow over your arm or attach it to the hook on a suitcase

____ Converter/transformer if you are traveling internationally

____ Passport or other travel documents for international travel

____ Tickets

____ Reading materials and journals—if you put them in lock-top bags, they are protected and slide in and out of side pockets of suitcases more easily

____ Jewelry—in a fabric jewelry case

____ Envelopes, stamps

____ Camera and film

$ How to Save Dollars for Family Fun

● Evaluate how much you need in accommodations. Do you need to stay in a $150-a-night suite in a hotel? If the hotel itself is your destination and you want to lie around the pool and spend most of your time right there, then get a package deal for an upscale hotel and stay there. If you just need a bed and a clean room, then get economy accommodations.

● Book early to get the best deals on everything: flights, cruises, hotels.

Evaluate how you will save money on food. Don't feed your family fast food every meal. Their stomachs will be upset, and if the diet has a lot of sugar, your kids will be wild. Feed them basically the same way you eat at home. On long drives, stock a cooler with fruits, ready-to-eat veggies, and precooked chicken, turkey, etc. from the local grocery store. Avoid a lot of highly sugared drinks. Purchase fruit juice and flavored water, or even better, let the kids drink plain water. Buy paper plates, napkins, and hand sanitizer for cleaning up before meals. Then stop at roadside rest areas and city parks for meals. Let the kids run and play for a while. (Toys such as Frisbees and balls don't take up much space in the car but provide lots of energy-burning activity while you are preparing a meal.) Feeding your family this way will save a lot of money over eating all your meals in restaurants, and it's better for them.

- If you want to eat in a nice restaurant but save money, think about breakfast. Breakfast is the cheapest meal of the day in

> **If you want to eat in a nice restaurant but save money, think about breakfast.**

restaurants, and you can get some wonderful meals that are more like lunch than breakfast.

- Find out all the free things you can do in the area where you are headed. Almost every city in the United States has a website and lists the attractions for that area. Make yourself a notebook and insert pages printed from the web that give sites of interest at your destination or along the way.

- Subscribe to *Budget Travel* magazine. For great online savings on your subscription, just type the name of the magazine in your search engine.

let's go camping

Many American families with young children have discovered the joy of camping vacations. These can build wonderful memories. They are well worth the effort, time, and money invested to make them work. But they can also be difficult if you have not prepared well, so plan ahead carefully by following the steps and checklists in this chapter. Then you will be able to approach a family camping vacation with anticipation and expectation that this is going to be a great time for all of you. Have a wonderful time together in the great outdoors.

233

Levels of Camping

Let's start at expensive camping and work our way down to inexpensive.

1. *Recreational vehicles.* Some of them are living proof that "you can take it with you." The really big RVs have everything from a bathroom with a tub and/or shower to plush carpet in a lovely living room. Other RVs are more modest and basically provide a place to sleep and cook. Either kind of RV, while very comfortable, demands maintenance of both the living area and the vehicle underneath. Weigh carefully how much of your life and money you want to spend caring for an RV. Then there is the exorbitant amount of fuel these vehicles use and the parking, licensing, and dumping fees that come with them. You also have to have a place to store an RV when it is not in use. Only your family knows if this kind of camping is right for you and your pocketbook.

2. *Camper trailers.* A step down, but still very nice, are camper trailers you pull behind a vehicle. These provide a place to sleep (usually for four to six people), cook food, and get away from insects and out of inclement weather. They are small in overall floor space, so much of your living will be done outside the camper. You will also have to pay licensing

234

fees and for a storage place if you do not have space at your home.

3. *Tent trailers.* Another rung down the expense ladder are tent trailers. These are basically tents on wheels. Most tent trailers pop up in one fashion or another. The "tent" part is, of course, soft sided and does not provide as much protection from the elements as a hard-sided vehicle. But you are up off the ground, and once your trailer is parked and the tent popped up, you can be quite comfortable. Again there are licensing fees and storage considerations.

4. *Yurts.* Then there are yurts, the tent houses patterned after Mongolian dwellings. These "tents" are larger and more complex to set up than ordinary tents. Since they are semi-permanently installed over a wooden floor, they are not practical for a family on the move. They would best be set up at family-owned property where they could stay up for the whole vacation season. State parks often have yurts to rent. In these yurts, you may find electrical outlets, a heater, beds covered with vinyl mattresses where you can toss a sleeping bag, and electric lights. They have vents at the top to allow heated air to escape in hot weather. Because yurts are so snug, you can extend the camping season by several months. The downside is that all cooking must be done outside the yurt, and that can be a chilly job in November.

5. *Tents.* There are dozens, probably hundreds, of styles of tents. These days they are light, waterproof, and come with all kinds of amenities, such as screened rooms, storage areas, and hanging pockets to keep keys and glasses off the floor. There are big tents, little tents, and everything in-between. There

are two-man tents and tents that will sleep a dozen. You pick. Humanity has been living in tents since the beginning of time, and the science of tent making has been refined to make tenting more comfortable than you might imagine. If you refrain from taking along more than you actually need, you can probably get by with hauling all of your tenting equipment in a cartop carrier or even in the trunk of your car or the back of your SUV, eliminating the need for a trailer.

Why Go Camping?

There are lots of wonderful reasons for camping as a family. Let's talk about some of them.

1. *Inexpensive.* Once your equipment is purchased, camping is probably one of the least expensive of all vacations. Equipment can be bought secondhand through thrift shops, second-time-around sporting goods stores, Ebay, and the classified ads. As much as families love camping, there comes a day when the equipment is no longer needed, and they sell it for next to nothing.

236

2. *Close to nature.* No other kind of vacation puts you as close to nature as camping does. Setting up a tent beside a mountain stream, in a desert, or beside the ocean provides an adventure your children will never forget.

3. *Teaches problem solving.* No matter how carefully you plan for your camping trip, something will go wrong. It always does. Hopefully what goes wrong is only inconvenient and not dangerous. Every new camping area has its adventures and challenges. Children can learn a lot by helping you figure out how to make something work, how to find something, or how to fix something.

> **Setting up a tent beside a mountain stream, in a desert, or beside the ocean provides an adventure your children will never forget.**

4. *Provides a time for communication.* Camping provides an opportunity for families to talk. While you can put a television in an RV or tent trailer, or perhaps even in a yurt, it would be so much better if your family could take a vacation from television as well. Camping is a great time to read books or play board or card games together. Many campgrounds have evening educational programs, sometimes with slide shows that your family might enjoy. Whatever you choose to do, be sure to encourage talk between family members, because it is the best way to get to know one another better.

5. *Provides multiple activities.* Many camping facilities have hiking, fishing, swimming, and biking facilities. Check the location where you plan to camp to see what it has and what equipment is available to rent. Not having to take these items with you will be a big help in conserving space.

Where to Go

1. *National parks.* These are a national treasure and one that families should try to enjoy together. From the grandeur of Yosemite to the amazing thermal activity of Yellowstone to the endless beauty of Great Smoky Mountains National Park, your family will be amazed at the natural wonders God has given us in this land. Be sure to book ahead at http://reservations.nps.gov/index.cfm. Read up on what is in

From the grandeur of Yosemite to the amazing thermal activity of Yellowstone to the endless beauty of Great Smoky Mountains National Park, your family will be amazed at the natural wonders God has given us in this land.

the park you will be visiting that will expand your children's thinking and life experience.

2. *State parks.* There is a website for each state. Go to your search engine and put in a destination state and the word "camping." Then go to your selected state's individual website and follow instructions for reserving space.

3. *National forests.* National forests are more primitive than state parks, but getting a reservation in one is usually easier and less expensive. Here is the website where you can make reservations: http://www.reserveusa.com/.

4. *Commercial sites.* One of the best known of the commercial camping sites is Kampgrounds of America (KOA). Although the campgrounds are usually packed during the summer, they are well operated and seem to be just about everywhere. You may even find them in the middle of a tourist area or in the heart of a city. Just be sure to make reservations ahead of time during peak travel seasons at http://www.koakamp grounds.com/where/usa .htm.

5. *Camping clubs.* If you plan to do a lot of camping, especially with a travel trailer

239

or RV, then perhaps a camping club membership would be best for your family. This website gives a lot of helpful information about camping clubs and camping in general: http://camping.about .com/.

6. *Primitive camping.* Primitive camping is not for the fainthearted, nor for the inexperienced camper. I have friends who would not think of camping in any of the facilities listed above. Their idea of camping is to go out in the woods somewhere, pitch a tent, dig a latrine, and either try to find a spring or another water source or bring water with them. Not only is this the tough way to camp, but the camper has to know the rules about fires and fire danger, wild animals in the area, poisonous snakes, and disposal of garbage. If there are no garbage receptacles, you have to take your garbage home to dispose of it.

7. *Backpack camping.* I don't put backpack camping in the same league with primitive camping. There are some places on earth you can never get to unless you backpack to them, and they are some of the most splendid places you will ever see. My

240

experience in backpacking is limited to a couple of trips into the Bob Marshall Wilderness in Montana.

My advice for backpacking is simple.

- You carry it in and you carry it out. There are no motorized vehicles to rescue you if you get tired on backpacking adventures.

- Be in condition before you attempt carrying a pack all day long.

- Register where you are going with the appropriate authorities.

- Let friends and family know where you are going and when you will return.

- Find out about dangerous animals in the area where you will be hiking and decide how you will deal with an encounter.

- Streamline your operation so that you are not carrying one thing more than you will need.

- Include a first-aid kit in your pack. Wounded feet are probably the greatest problem, so take moleskin or other foot products to ease blisters and treat hot spots on your feet at the first indication of a problem.

- Cover the areas on your feet that you know are likely to blister (for example, the back of your heels) with a

241

strip of duct tape. This prevents blisters—your hiking boot now rubs against the tape rather than your skin. (And speaking of hiking boots, it's always a good idea to wear them.)

- Take some short backpack hikes to learn how to do it. One day in and one day out will teach you a lot about how to do this kind of camping.

- An awesome website for backpacking, sponsored by REI and including articles from *Outdoor* magazine, is http://gorp.away.com/index.html. You have to register, but it is free.

Let's Go Camping Checklist

Here is a list of the basic equipment needed for a camping trip.

■ *Sleeping Gear*

____ sleeping bags

____ foam pads, rolled up, or air mattresses

242

_____ small pillows in dark-colored cases

_____ air pump, if using air mattresses

_____ flashlights

■ Cooking Gear

_____ stove

_____ propane tank

_____ stove lighter

_____ matches

_____ ten-inch frying pan

_____ three nesting cooking
pots

243

___ locking pliers

___ pancake turner

___ large spoon

___ vinyl tablecloth

___ tongs

___ pot holders

___ sticks for campfire cooking

___ ice chest

___ serrated knife

___ enamel dishpans

___ detergent

___ scouring pad

___ water container

___ thermos

___ can opener

___ lock-top bags

◾ *Food Staples*

___ salt and pepper

___ small amount of flour

___ small amount of sugar

___ shortening

___ oil

___ menu items

◾ *Plates and Utensils*

___ paper plates

___ rattan plate holders

245

_____ paper napkins or paper towels

_____ thermal cups

_____ nesting glasses

_____ silverware

_____ small plastic bowls with lids

■ *Clothing*

_____ rain gear

_____ stocking caps

_____ jackets

_____ wool sweaters

_____ swimsuits

_____ shoes

_____ personal clothing

_____ clothesline and pins

■ *Linens*

___ small rug for in front of the tent door

___ dishtowels

___ dishcloths

___ towels

___ washcloths

■ *Toiletries*

___ toothbrushes

___ toothpaste

247

_____ hairbrush

_____ personal items

_____ soap

_____ mirror

_____ first-aid items

_____ toilet paper with core removed to conserve space

_____ shampoo

_____ bug spray

_____ sunscreen

■ *Add for Tent Camping*

_____ tent with a covering tarp

_____ tent poles and stakes

_____ waterproof tarp for a
ground cloth

____ ax or hammer
for pounding stakes

____ rope to tie tent down in
case of strong wind

____ whiskbroom to clean feet
before entering the tent

▧ *Bikes, Fun, and Games*

____ bikes

____ bike rack

____ lock and chain

____ Frisbee

____ kite

____ games

____ books

249

Easy Tips for Campers

Save money on food for your trip by planning your menus far ahead and then watching the store ads for the best deals.

Instead of money- and time-saving tips, for this chapter I want to share with you some of my personal camping tips. I learned these first-hand over a period of many years. Some of them will save money and some will save time, and others are just good to know.

First of all, you need to know that I am a lazy camper. My attitude is that I didn't come camping to work harder than I would have to at home. And I can only go without a shower for a couple days. To top it off, I want to sleep in comfort. So here's how I do it.

▨ *Meals*

I always make it a policy to fix the same kind of food while camping that the family eats at home. Picnic food is all right for one or two meals, but on an extended vacation, it can cause all kinds of problems. So cook meals similar to those you eat at home.

1. *Invest in a good propane camp stove with a good-sized fuel tank.* The stove I had folded up to the size of a briefcase, and the large tank of propane would last for an entire trip.

2. *Plan your menus ahead of time.* Plan a lot of one-dish dinners. Topped off with a piece of fruit, a cookie, and something to drink, these will make a great evening meal.

3. *Prepackage all the food items you will need for your menu.* Take food items out of boxes and put the food in lock-top plastic bags. Be sure to tuck the cooking directions into the bag. You will be amazed at how much room you save by getting rid of the packaging. I like to put all those smaller bags of items for a meal into a larger lock-top bag and put a piece of paper in the big bag that has the day the items are to be used.

4. *Plan to stop at a grocery store late in the afternoon (assuming you will be near a grocery store) to purchase fresh meat.* This is also a great time to replenish your ice supply for the cooler.

5. *Always have one or two planned backup meals* using canned meats in case you cannot get to a grocery store. Canned chicken, tuna, corned beef, and salmon can be worked into one-dish meals.

6. *Make breakfast and lunch at the same time.* Breakfast might be a bowl of cereal or an omelet or pancakes. Get a family member to flip the pancakes or stir the eggs while you get out bread and make sandwiches. Slip the prepared sandwiches into sandwich bags and tuck them in the cooler. Then, wherever you may be at lunch time, just get them out and pass them around. After everyone has eaten breakfast,

you can clean up from both breakfast and lunch preparation, and you are through with food until evening.

7. *Use paper plates.* Get the really cheap ones. Buy a rattan or plastic plate holder for each member of the family and insert paper plates in them for meals. The holder will keep the paper plate from blowing away and provide stability. Because the plates are so inexpensive, family members can have a new one for each course. If the rattan becomes soiled, it can be scrubbed, rinsed, and dried.

8. *Use real flatware instead of plasticware.* I don't like the bending and breaking that happens when you use plastic knives and forks. So if you choose to use flatware, it will have to be stored and washed. I store mine in an empty potato chip can that has a lid. Put the points of forks and knives downward in the can to avoid being pricked by them. Store the spoons bowl up; they will be easier to find that way. To save money, pick up a set of flatware (or make up a set from odds and ends) at a thrift shop and run it through the dishwasher to clean it.

9. *Doing dishes.* Of course, doing dishes with paper plates simply means disposing of them in the proper trash receptacles. But for any other cooking implements, I use two small enamel pans. I put one on each burner of the stove, fill them with water, and light the fire under them to warm the water. Turn the fire off when the water reaches the right temperature. Then I wash and rinse the dishes and put them in a net bag (like the ones from the grocery store that hold oranges) and hang the bag up. When you are ready for another meal, the dishes will be dry.

10. *Save money on food* for your trip by planning your menus far ahead and then watching the store ads for the best deals. Prepackaged dinners to which you can add chicken or crumbled hamburger are expensive unless you pick them up on sale.

11. *Watch for sales on packets of one-serving foods* such as soup, hot breakfast cereals, granola bars, trail mix, hot chocolate drinks, iced tea, and other drinks. Anything that can be prepared simply by adding hot water is a good thing to have along for snacks.

12. *Let your kids help* you plan the meals and do that prepackaging. It's great training. And as soon as they are able to cook over a camp stove or campfire, let them.

13. *Allow flexibility in your vacation budget* for those days when you just can't cook outside, due to inclement weather or because you've traveled too far and are tired. Go eat in a restaurant.

14. *Instead of serving desserts*, plan to stop at ice cream or frozen yogurt shops or fresh fruit stands. The stop makes a nice memory, and this also gives a break from camp food.

15. *A caution for parents*: be sure that your kids are careful around campground fire pits. Coals and ashes from your fire the night before can still be hot through the next day, and children who fall into the fire pit may be seriously burned.

quick guide to
saving money

Three areas of huge money and time expenditures are those of feeding a family, clothing them, and decorating your home so that it is comfortable for your family. Here is a quick guide to help you cut down on expenses, save time doing it, and figure out how to do both by giving you ideas for do-it-yourself projects.

Food

■ *What to Buy*

● Buy eggs. If your cholesterol level can handle it, eggs are a good source of protein and are usually cheap.

● Buy the least expensive kind of cheddar cheese for cooking. Buy a better cheese for snacking.

● Buy skim milk for cooking. It's better for you and cheaper than reconstituted dry milk.

● Buy generic or store brands. If you have a question as to their quality, buy one and try it. If it meets your standard, stock up on the next trip. What you are not paying for is a lot of advertising.

● Buy "raw" food whenever possible. Remember that every time someone does something to your food, it adds to the cost. Besides that, you don't know what has been added. Prepackaged, precooked, prebreaded, pre-anything adds dollars to your food bill. And raw food is better for your health.

● Pancakes made from a dry mix are cheaper than frozen pancakes and cheaper than a ready-pour mix.

● Buy seasonal fruits and vegetables. Not only are they less expensive, they also taste better when they are at

the peak of the season. Melons picked in midsummer always taste better than the first and most expensive ones that appear in supermarkets in the spring.

- If possible, teach your kids to eat whole-grain cereals such as oatmeal and other cooked grains. They are more nutritious and less expensive. Remember that taste is acquired, so kids can be taught new eating habits.

- Buy a low-fat variety of popcorn instead of chips. It's much cheaper, less fattening if you stick with low-fat varieties and don't add butter, and better for you.

- Check different forms of a certain food—fresh, frozen, canned—to see which is the best buy. Do not assume one form is always cheaper than another.

- Some of the less expensive cuts of meat can also be the most flavorful but must be prepared properly to tenderize them.

- Buy boneless meat cuts whenever possible. Pound for pound, they're cheaper.

■ *Where to Buy*

- Watch dairy case close-out areas for marked-down milk, eggs, cottage cheese, cheese, and juices. Sometimes they are less than half-price, and many have not yet reached the expiration date.

- Buy directly from the growers whenever possible for the freshest produce. A sign on a strawberry stand near my house reads, "Our berries slept in our fields last night." That's fresh.

> **A sign on a strawberry stand near my house reads, "Our berries slept in our fields last night." That's fresh.**

● Limit purchases of perishable foods, even when they are a great bargain. You are not saving money if the excess has to be thrown out.

● Chain discount stores will often have lower prices on many foods.

■ *How to Shop*

● Always use a shopping list and stick to it.

● Buy only what you need, but be sure to buy everything you need for a particular dish. That way you will not have to go back for more ingredients. Every trip to the supermarket causes you to spend added gasoline costs, added food dollars, and added time. How many times have you gone for one item and come out with a bagful of food?

● Don't shop when you are tired or hungry or when the store is crowded, because you won't be able to think through your purchases.

- Use coupons, but be careful not to buy more expensive items just because you have a coupon. Think it through before buying. Some stores offer double savings on coupons, and if you can combine a sale and a coupon, you can make significant savings.

Do-It-Yourself

- Remember that extra packaging raises prices. Buy huge bags of potato chips and repackage in smaller plastic bags for school lunches. (They freeze well.) Buy a large container of instant oatmeal, rather than small packets.

- Buy cheese in bulk and spend a few minutes shredding it for topping casseroles and other dishes. For extra convenience, package it in the amount needed for one dish. Cheese can be frozen if it is to be used for cooking.

- Buy potatoes, carrots, onions, and grapefruit in large sacks. They are considerably cheaper than the individual items.

- Grind your own coffee at the store and save, but stay away from gourmet coffee beans if you want to save money.

- Buy raisins in two-pound (or larger) bags and repackage for snacks.

- If you toss a salad with dressing before serving it, you will use less dressing than if it is served separately. Because dressings add calories, this is a great way to cut down on fat in your diet and save money.

- Vegetables frozen in butter and those with other added seasonings and ingredients are nearly twice the price of the plain ones. By adding your own butter and herbs, you can save big.

- Nothing could be easier to make than the new muffin mixes, and they are cheap and delicious. Buy them instead of fresh muffins from the bakery counter.

- Use up leftover meat and poultry by grinding it in a food processor with onions, a dash of Worcestershire sauce, mustard, and mayonnaise for a hearty sandwich spread.

- Sliver pork, chicken, or beef leftovers and stir-fry with fresh vegetables.

- Crumble meat loaf and add it to spaghetti sauce or vegetable soup.

- Boil turkey bones to make a delicious broth as a soup base. After the turkey is boiled, every scrap of meat can be removed from the bones and added to the soup stock.

- Bits and pieces of ham or turkey can be added to an ordinary salad to turn it into a great chef's salad.

- Sliver cold, leftover roast beef and serve it as a side dish. Hot Chinese mustard and sesame seeds for dipping make it special.

- Add cooked leftover vegetables to omelets.

- Keep a stock pot in the refrigerator as a place to recycle leftover vegetables and meats. Either freeze them or use them to make soup after a few days.

- Mash up the inside of leftover baked potatoes with a little milk until fluffy. Pile the potato back into the skin; top with cheese, bacon bits, and onions; and reheat in the microwave.

- Cook sliced onion in butter or margarine until just tender. Then add sliced leftover potatoes. Heat through. Add shredded cheese, put a lid on the pan, and remove it from the heat. In a few minutes the cheese will be melted into the potatoes.

- Serve leftover spaghetti cold as an oriental salad. Use a little soy sauce for seasoning and add some sesame seeds.

- Make croutons from dry bread.

- Turn dry bread into crumbs by chopping it in the blender. These are great browned in butter and sprinkled over vegetables.

- Make an elegant English trifle using leftover cake—preferably stale pound or angel food cake. Layer cake with peaches or raspberries, custard pudding, whipped cream, and toasted almonds, all in a large, clear glass bowl.

- Learn to eat simple desserts such as fruit and cookies, puddings, and frozen yogurt, rather than more expensive pies and cakes.

- Use old-fashioned rice that has to be cooked for twenty minutes, rather than instant rice that takes five minutes and costs twice as much. You can probably afford the extra fifteen minutes, and you can make rice pudding with the leftovers.

- Teach your kids to make cinnamon toast instead of filling up on cupcakes and other filled pastries. Mix some sugar and cinnamon in a shaker and make this treat easier for children to fix.

- Buy food in large containers if your family can consume it before it spoils. It is usually considerably cheaper (and more environmentally sound) than several small containers. Compare prices.

- Serve less meat and mix it with vegetables, pastas, rice, and breads to make a little go further. Or prepare meatless meals a couple of times a week. Use eggs, cheese, beans, dry peas, and peanut butter as a protein source on those days.

● Remove the fat from meat drippings and use the rest of the juices to flavor gravies, soups, and sauces rather than buying packaged seasonings and gravies.

● When fruits and vegetables are at their peak, think about freezing some for use later on. Broccoli is very cheap at certain times of the year. All you need to do is wash it thoroughly, blanch it in hot water for a couple minutes, cool it under cold running water, and package it for the freezer.

Clothing

■ *What to Buy*

Whether you are buying brand-new clothing or thrift-shop clothing, you need a checklist to evaluate how substantial the garment is.

Checklist for Clothing

● Buy the best quality you can afford. It lasts longer. Learn what quality is and look for brand-name labels at discount prices. Some discount stores, such as Target and Wal-Mart, have well-made children's clothing at excellent prices, especially if you check sale racks and look for advertised specials.

● Check tags for fiber content. Natural fibers—wool, cotton, silk—can't be beat for wearability, packability, and holding their shape.

● Look for the care label and see if this garment requires dry cleaning. If it does, don't buy it. Dry cleaning is too costly for those who are trying to save money on clothing.

● Check seams and hems of garments. Skimpy seams are a mark of inferior construction. Make sure the seams are not puckered.

● If the fabric is permanent press, you won't be able to let out seams or let down hems without the seam mark showing. Creases on permanent-pressed garments are permanent.

● The zipper should lie flat with no puckers around it. The zipper's teeth should match the color of the garment.

● If the piece is lined, is the lining of good quality and does it match the outer fabric? Well-made dresses and pants are lined.

● Are the buttons good-looking? Buttons are the jewelry of an outfit. Nothing says shoddy quicker than cheap-looking buttons. However, buttons can be replaced. So if the garment is great, buy it and get new buttons.

- Buttonholes should be well made with no threads hanging loose. The thread color should match the color of the garment.

- The lapels of a garment should lie flat. The top layer of fabric should not be bonded to the lapel, as they will separate and pucker after a time.

- Do the seams at the underarm meet exactly?

- Do plaids and stripes match evenly where the sleeve and the garment are joined?

Buy simple, durable clothing and accessorize with scarves, jackets, and jewelry for a completely different look. New ties and shirts for guys will give suits a whole new look.

■ *Where to Buy*

- Buy great clothing at garage sales, thrift stores, outlets, resale shops, and discount stores. Some of these shopping trips might make a great family adventure.

- Watch for big-name store sales and be there when the door opens.

265

● Shop season-ending sales. Summer and winter will come again next year.

■ Do-It-Yourself

● If you can sew, learn to make simple garments to save money. But if you plan to save money by sewing, you have to consider the value of your time. Also, fabrics and notions for sewing can be expensive. Watch closeout bins at fabric stores as well as remnant bins for fabric pieces. There are some great bargains among these things.

> **If you plan to save money by sewing, you have to consider the value of your time.**

● Even if you don't sew, learn to mend. Kids have a way of going through clothing like a hot knife through butter. Here are some simple mending tasks that will give you and your children more clothes to wear.

a. Sew on buttons. Some sewing machines will sew on buttons with holes that go all the way through. Find out if your machine will. If you are hand-sewing on buttons, find a needle that has an eye small enough to fit through the button but big enough to accommodate four or eight strands of thread. Using eight strands of thread means fewer times through the holes of the button and therefore makes the whole operation faster.

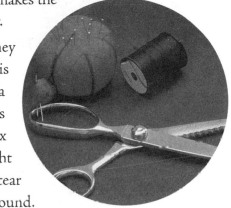

b. Fix hems as soon as they start to come out. This is one place where "a stitch in time saves nine." If you don't fix it right away, you might step on the hem and tear it loose all the way around.

c. The same goes for seams. If you catch a seam that has come open because a few stitches have popped, it only takes a minute to fix it—easier than fixing a foot-long open seam.

d. Fix small tears in kids' clothing by covering the tear with a decorative iron-on patch and then sewing around the edge to keep the patch from coming loose.

e. Men's pants can be taken in and let out for a better fit.

- Buy inexpensive costume jewelry to dress up an outfit.

- Dress up plain pumps with shoe clips.

- Learn how to remove stains from children's clothing.

- Shop in your closets. Do you even know what's in there?

a. Take everything out.

b. Evaluate what fits, what works for you, and what you like. Keep those garments.

c. Toss everything else (or add pieces that would make a fun costume to your costume trunk).

d. Repair, restyle, retrofit, and clean everything you want to keep. Voilà! A whole new wardrobe that works.

e. Make a rule: nothing gets put away that is not ready to wear at a moment's notice.

Home Decorating

■ What to Buy

● Buy only what you need.

● Buy the best quality you can afford.

● Buy durable finishes and fabrics.

■ Where to Buy

● Buy furniture through classified ads. Check these headings: garage sales, moving sales, relocation sales, and estate sales.

● Look in resale and consignment shops that sell furniture and home-decorating accessories.

268

- Look for warehouse sales—one-of-a-kind or closeout models.

- Visit auctions, but be careful. Know what you are buying, since you won't be able to bring it back. Attend and watch and learn before you bid.

- High-quality furniture stores have excellent sales several times a year. Save your money and pay cash for the best savings.

■ Do-It-Yourself

- Buy unfinished furniture and finish it yourself. With the popularity of painted furniture, this is a great way to get custom-made pieces. Attend a paint class at a large discount store such as Home Depot or Lowes or search decorating magazines for instructions.

- Slipcover old furniture. If you can sew, you can make slipcovers. If you can't, there are many places to buy ready-made slipcovers. You can slipcover dining-room chairs for a charming, fresh look.

- Make new throw pillows, curtains, or floor-length table skirts to dress up old furniture.

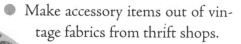

- Build your own furniture.

- Make accessory items out of vintage fabrics from thrift shops.

- Use tea towels or cotton kerchiefs to cover throw pillows.

- Paint stools in bright colors for the kitchen.

- Paint walls with a sponging or ragging method. This covers many imperfections in the walls.

- Paint terra-cotta pots in matching colors for a color splash in the kitchen, porch, or patio.

- Paint galvanized buckets (or buy colored ones) for storing small toys such as Legos, crayons, and small action figures. Or use the painted buckets outdoors for a splash of inexpensive color.

- Use gift-wrapping paper to cover badly damaged furniture or even an old trunk. Glue on the gift wrap and cover it with several coats of varnish for an indestructible surface.

- Paint your wooden floor with a checkerboard design or faux carpet.

- Paint a checkerboard design on an outdoor table.

270

- Think about making your own toppers, café curtains, and sheer curtains. Put them on lovely rods available inexpensively everywhere.

- Think upward—look for ways to use your doors and walls for storage space. Put a bookshelf at the top of the room or hang racks on doors as places to store shoes and magazines.

- Use lots of inexpensive fabric when decorating. It gives a sumptuous look, and sheets are the least expensive decorating material.

- Use a section of picket fence in front of the fireplace for a fresh summer look when the fireplace will not be in use. Bank the fence with real or silk flowers and greenery.

- Cover damaged walls with fabric. Padding stapled to the walls behind the fabric will give the walls a posh look. Cover seams with decorative trim.

- Pad and upholster a headboard of a bed to coordinate with the bedspread and other fabrics used in the room.

fifty ideas for free family fun

1. Check out videos from the local library for an evening of video fun. Popular videos disappear early from library shelves. Make sure you have the one you want at the time you want it by reserving early.

2. See if your library has art prints to check out. Bring them home and hang them at your house. Try to find out something about the artist and the picture.

3. Plan a family bike trip to a special destination—a park, a historic site, a lake, a special woods.

4. Organize a neighborhood basketball tournament at someone's house or at a local school or playground.

5. Find a factory to tour. If the factory only takes groups, gather up the neighborhood kids and their parents.

6. Go pick something found in the wild—apples, flowers, strawberries, asparagus, or blueberries. Do you even know what your area provides?

7. Go to a printing plant and watch the high-speed printing equipment. The printing process is fascinating.

8. Visit a shop or factory where candy is made. Especially interesting are the hand-dipped chocolates.

9. Collect bugs and identify them using a library book.

10. Find a small stream and build a dam across it. Splash about in the pool formed behind the dam. When you are finished, return everything to its natural state.

11. Go sledding or inner tubing with your kids.

12. Visit a television or radio station to see programming in action. In some areas it is possible to attend the taping of a show, and you can usually get free tickets. Simply go to Google and type in the name of the show. You will be able to get to the show's website where the ticket information is listed. Check to see if children are allowed at the tapings.

13. Play an old-fashioned game with your kids like Kick the Can or Hide and Seek. They'll love it.

14. Put together an old-fashioned radio drama with all the family participating. Record it and then play it back at a complete-with-popcorn family night.

15. Put up a tent in the yard and everyone sleeps out. Or use it to pretend you're on a safari or that you're pioneers moving west.

16. Read stories together in the dark by flashlight.

17. Check at museums to see what free workshops they are sponsoring. Take your kids so that all of you can learn.

18. Look for neighborhood story times at your local library or start one yourself for your neighborhood.

19. Go to a fish or salmon hatchery to see fingerlings or migrating salmon.

20. Teach a child a craft—knitting, crocheting, simple woodcraft, gardening.

21. Mix up a batch of salt dough and keep it in the refrigerator for impromptu projects.

    Here is the recipe for salt dough.

    > 2 cups white flour
    > ½ cup salt
    > Mix these two ingredients together and add
    >   ½ cup water slowly
    > Work the mixture into a dough
    > Knead for five minutes
    > Store in the refrigerator until ready to use
    >   for projects
    > Let the kids shape the dough
    > Bake at 250 degrees for 15–30 minutes
    > Paint with acrylic paints and finish with
    >   lacquer

22. Use Styrofoam meat trays for picture frames or let the kids weave colorful scrap yarn back and forth across the tray to form designs. They can use a large, dull-pointed

tapestry needle and actually punch through the edges of the Styrofoam tray.

23. Make fun hats out of paper plates and paper cups. Decorate using felt-tipped markers. Glue stickers, pom-poms, stars, buttons, or whatever you have lying about on the hats.

24. Make a pincushion. Here's how:

  ● Use pinking shears to cut two layers of fabric or felt in a variety of shapes.
  ● Let the kids sew the two layers together, joining the edges. Leave an opening for stuffing.
  ● Stuff with old nylon stockings or polyester filling.
  ● Sew the opening shut and attach a loop of ribbon or yarn for a hanger.

25. Get an out-of-date wallpaper book from a wallpaper shop. Cut out pieces with pinking shears and let the kids make their own greeting cards or book covers. Old wallpaper is also good for wrapping small gifts.

26. Go on a rock hunt. Pick up any interesting rocks and learn to classify them with the help of a good rock book from the library.

27. Let little kids play in the kitchen sink with soapy bubbles, an eggbeater, and other cooking implements. When they've finished, simply wipe up—it's a very clean game.

28. Cut pictures from old greeting cards to use as toppers on packages or use the pictures to make new greeting cards.

29. Set up an ant farm in a large glass jar. Find a book at the library to tell you more about doing this and more about ants in general.

30. In a container of dirt, plant various kinds of seeds from fruits and vegetables that you eat. Plant grapefruit, lemon, orange, squash, or apple seeds. If they are not a hybrid variety, they will come up. Suspend avocado seeds in water by inserting toothpicks in the sides to hold them in place. Do the same with various kinds of potatoes.

31. Make pictures by gluing various shapes of macaroni to cardboard. Paint with acrylic paints.

32. Make a calendar for grandma and grandpa by drawing twelve pictures and gluing them on another kind of calendar. Or on a copy machine, run twelve pages with a grid at the bottom for the dates and a space at the top for the children's pictures. Help them fill in the dates.

33. Make your own wrapping paper by block printing it with fruits and vegetables cut in half. Dip them in water-based poster paint and stamp the paper. Potatoes can be carved to shape, lemons and oranges make an interesting print, and half of an apple will work too.

34. Have a rhythm band using pot lids, wax paper fastened around combs (the children can hum to make an interesting sound), or beans in a milk jug for a shaker.

Put on some lively music and let the kids play to their hearts' content.

35. Take funnels, empty tin cans, sieves, shovels, trowels, and other implements to a sandy area. Build a fortress, a castle, and a tower. If the sand is dry, you'll need to add water to make it stick together.

36. Have the children see how many different kinds of something they can find: leaves, rocks, flowers, bugs, buttons, etc.

37. Let the children play store by getting out all the canned goods and lining them up in a display. Give them a handful of small change or provide them with play money. Let them use a muffin tin for a cash drawer. If they're old enough, help them begin to understand how to make change.

38. Have your children help you plan a vacation by sending for travel brochures and maps. Talk to them about how much money you will have to spend each day and enlist their ideas and help for making that money stretch far enough.

39. Let your children have a play. Collect costume materials for them and decide on a good place for them to put on their play. Be an enthusiastic audience when the time comes to watch the play.

40. Go to a stream. Skip rocks on the placid parts. Turn over rocks and see what's under them. Sit quietly and watch for birds such as kingfishers, water dippers, and

long-legged birds such as herons. Teach your children to be observant.

41. Walk in an empty lot and see if you can find useful discarded items. Use your imagination, together, to see if you can think of a way to use your finds. Remember, never limit an item to its original use.

42. Spend time together looking at old family photos and telling the children what was happening when those photos were taken.

43. Begin a family history by interviewing family members. Use a cassette recorder and get them to tell stories. Sometimes it helps older family members who might be intimidated by a tape recorder to be interviewed in a group. As one begins to talk, others add their viewpoints to the story. These tapes will be treasured in years to come when family members have died.

44. Find and save funny articles, cartoons, and photos to look at, laugh at, and read aloud. Laughter is good medicine for families.

45. Get a copy of Gladys Hunt's book *Honey for a Child's Heart* (Zondervan) and begin reading the recommended books listed in the back of the book. You can get the books from the library. Reading together as a family will build memories you'll treasure forever.

46. Have a family walkathon. Each person should select a walking distance goal according to his or her age. Post these on a chart by week or month. Have each family member record his or her daily walking record. See who

can come closest to or surpass his or her goal. This is great for promoting exercise.

47. Take turns planning and cooking meals. Remember, the planner and cook gets to choose anything he or she wants. This can be great creative fun and a help to busy parents too.

48. Let older kids go on a scavenger hunt. When they return with their treasures, have a special treat waiting for them—their favorite pizza or sundae.

49. Encourage older kids to have a garage sale. They should plan the day, do the advertising, collect the goods, mark the items, and plan what to do with the surplus. They should also be allowed to keep any money they make.

50. Check the back of appliance stores for a big box. Bring it home and turn it over to the kids. Watch their imagination take over.

the rest of the story

There you have it. A plan for having fun as a family, building memories no one can take from you, building traditions that will endure, nurturing creativity within your kids, having fun yourself, and a host of other good stuff.

Try It Out

If you have read this far in the book, you have more ideas than can possibly be used by one family in a lifetime. It doesn't really matter which part of the book you start with; just start. Do something and do it now. Make sure grandparents have a copy of the book, so that when kids come to their house, they'll have lots of great ideas ready. Remember when you used to go to grandma and grandpa's house and you were bored to death? Well, you don't have to hear that from your kids or grandkids. Grandparents have time to provide rich experiences for their grandkids, so get them a copy of this book to get their minds in gear.

Be sure to reread the chapter on traditions. Traditions are so important to family life, and the charts I've given you to fill out in that chapter are not just busywork. They will help you take the best ideas for your family from this book and build your own traditions. Filling out the sheets won't be time wasted; it will make *Simply Fun for Families* a truly useful tool.

Sit down with your kids tonight and decide on a time for reading together. Decide which books you'd like to read. You don't have to worry that you are picking the "correct" books; just find something you all like and read. Later on, your kids will hear about books in school, or they'll see a movie and want to know how it differs from the book, or their friends will tell them about a neat book they have read. Then you can read them the rest of the story at that time.

As for the money- and time-saving ideas, try them out. Everyone today is trying to save either time or money. You could become the authority on saving both. I assure you that if you put the money- and time-saving ideas I've given you to work, you will find extra time and save money. Let me encourage you to spend that time and money on your kids or grandkids. You will never be sorry for the investment you make in them. There are rich rewards for people who put their energies, talent, money, and time into other people. There is a harvest of love and appreciation far greater than you might imagine when you give of yourself to a child.

Whatever you do, embrace life. Embrace all of it. Give yourself 100 percent to what you do. Laugh a lot, cry a little, learn together, keep the faith in all you do. Life is good and passes by much too quickly. You probably have days when you wonder if your children will ever grow up. Yes, they will, and so will your grandchildren, and it could happen while you are looking the other way, distracted by the busyness of life.

> **There is a harvest of love and appreciation far greater than you might imagine when you give of yourself to a child.**

A Blessed Woman

Your author is a blessed woman. I grew up in the mountains of Montana and lived a very simple life of hard work, strong faith, consistent discipline, and tons of fun with Mom and Dad. We went fishing in Montana's bubbling rivers and brooks. We skated over frozen ponds and warmed ourselves by the fires Dad built on the ice. We played sports, and Mom and Dad were always in the stands. We performed in concerts, and there they were. We acted in school plays, and yes, you guessed. Back about two or three rows, there were Mom and Dad, proud as peacocks.

We traveled, and Dad made sure we saw the biggest and the best. He put us on a speedboat for a ride around Flathead Lake. We toured Grand Coulee Dam; we saw Yellowstone and Glacier national parks; we visited the Corn Palace in Mitchell, South Dakota; we saw the passion play in the Black Hills; and we thought we were rich folks traveling around. As fun as all that travel was, what I remember most were our camping trips. I thought they were big excursions, but often they were to a place twenty or thirty miles from home where Dad could fish, Mom could attempt to read (if we'd leave her alone long enough), and we kids could play in the water and then dry out at the campfire.

Mom and Dad didn't read out loud to us a lot, but Dad read fairly consistently and always told us what he was reading. It made me hungry to know more. He also talked and talked about ideas and inventions he wanted to make. Mom made sure I had a library card when I was very young and encouraged me to read. I don't know if she realized that many times I read almost all night long. If she did, she never scolded me.

And we had traditions. Mom was a fabulous cook and loved to throw dinner parties. If you stopped by at meal time, you were invited to eat with us. Mom's Thanksgiving and Christmas dinners were legendary, with fabulous food, beautiful dishes, centerpieces, cloth napkins, the whole bit. Often on Thanksgiving, she would put dinner in the oven, and we would go to the mountains for a while before coming back to dinner. She fixed a gorgeous dinner even if it was just the five of us.

Life was hard at times in Montana. Workers at the smelter where Dad worked would strike, sometimes for weeks. Dad injured his back and had to go to Seattle for back surgery. He was off work for months. Money was scarce during those times, but we never feared going hungry.

Dad always planted a big garden and we all got involved in the harvest and preservation of that harvest. I've strung more green beans and slipped the skins off more tomatoes and dug more potatoes than I care to remember. And guess what? It didn't hurt me a bit. Mom and Dad both hunted, and we ate every morsel of the meat, and Dad sold the hides. Dad fished for trout, and they both fished for sockeye salmon. They picked wild huckleberries (you haven't lived until you've eaten warm huckleberry pie with ice cream), and they bought raw honey by the five-gallon can.

We made our clothes and our quilts. We did our own repairs and never hired anyone to fix a roof or mow the grass. And we made our own fun. We had dramatic plays for our family. We played board games. We played outdoor games of running and skill together as a family. We didn't watch much television because it didn't come to our valley until I was in high school, and I am very glad.

We buried Dad about five years ago and Mom just a few months ago while I was still writing this book. I miss them so much, but I carry within me their legacy—a legacy of trust, thrift, common sense, can-do, and simple, free fun. Give your kids what my folks gave me, what I tried to give my children, and now what I hope to be involved in giving my grandchildren.

Gwen Ellis lives in California, where after retiring she started her own business, Seaside Creative Services. Gwen writes, speaks, and consults with publishing companies. Learn more at www.seasidecreativeservices.com.